Praise for *Inside the Minds*

"What C-Level executives read to keep their edge and make pivotal business decisions. Timeless classics for indispensable knowledge." - Richard Costello, Manager -Corporate Marketing Communication, General Electric (NYSE: GE)

"Want to know what the real leaders are thinking about now? It's in here."- Carl Ledbetter, SVP & CTO, Novell, Inc.

"Priceless wisdom from experts at applying technology in support of business objectives." - Frank Campagnoni, CTO, GE Global Exchange Services

"Unique insights into the way the experts think and the lessons they've learned from experience." - MT Rainey, Co-CEO, Young & Rubicam/Rainey Kelly Campbell Roalfe

"Unlike any other business book." - Bruce Keller, Partner, Debevoise & Plimpton

"The Inside the Minds series is a valuable probe into the thought, perspectives, and techniques of accomplished professionals. By taking a 50,000 foot view, the authors place their endeavors in a context rarely gleaned from text books or treatise." - Chuck Birenbaum, Partner, Thelen Reid & Priest

"A must read for anyone in the industry." - Dr. Chuck Lucier, Chief Growth Officer, Booz-Allen & Hamilton

"A must read for those who manage at the intersection of business and technology." - Frank Roney, General Manager, IBM

"A great way to see across the changing marketing landscape at a time of significant innovation." - David Kenny, Chairman & CEO, Digitas

"An incredible resource of information to help you develop outside-the-box..." - Rich Jernstedt, CEO, Golin/Harris International

"A snapshot of everything you need..." - Charles Koob, Co-Head of Litigation Department, Simpson Thacher & Bartlet

www.Aspatore.com

Aspatore Books is the largest and most exclusive publisher of C-Level executives (CEO, CFO, CTO, CMO, Partner) from the world's most respected companies and law firms. Aspatore annually publishes a select group of C-Level executives from the Global 1,000, top 250 law firms (Partners and Chairs), and other leading companies of all sizes. C-Level Business Intelligence™, as conceptualized and developed by Aspatore Books, provides professionals of all levels with proven business intelligence from industry insiders – direct and unfiltered insight from those who know it best – as opposed to third-party accounts offered by unknown authors and analysts. Aspatore Books is committed to publishing an innovative line of business and legal books, those which lay forth principles and offer insights that when employed, can have a direct financial impact on the reader's business objectives, whatever they may be. In essence, Aspatore publishes critical tools – need-to-read as opposed to nice-to-read books – for all business professionals.

Inside the Minds

The critically acclaimed *Inside the Minds* series provides readers of all levels with proven business intelligence from C-Level executives (CEO, CFO, CTO, CMO, Partner) from the world's most respected companies. Each chapter is comparable to a white paper or essay and is a future-oriented look at where an industry/profession/topic is heading and the most important issues for future success. Each author has been carefully chosen through an exhaustive selection process by the *Inside the Minds* editorial board to write a chapter for this book. *Inside the Minds* was conceived in order to give readers actual insights into the leading minds of business executives worldwide. Because so few books or other publications are actually written by executives in industry, *Inside the Minds* presents an unprecedented look at various industries and professions never before available.

Inside the Minds:

The Insurance Business

Industry Leaders on Managing Risks, Ensuring Investments, & Protecting Assets

Published by Aspatore, Inc.

For corrections, company/title updates, comments or any other inquiries please e-mail info@aspatore.com.

First Printing, 2004
10 9 8 7 6 5 4 3 2 1

ISBN 1-58762-423-0 Library of Congress Control Number: 2004113887

Inside the Minds Managing Editor, Laura Kearns, Edited by Marissa Berenson, Proofread by Eddie Fournier, Cover design by Scott Rattray and Ian Mazie

Inside the Minds:
The Insurance Business
Industry Leaders on Managing Risks, Ensuring
Investments, & Protecting Assets

CONTENTS

The Business of Managing Risks

Martin D. Feinstein, CPCU, CLU, GCA

Chairman of the Board & Chief Executive Officer
Farmers Group, Inc.

Insurance Business Basics

The concept of insurance is a simple one, yet difficult for many to comprehend. It is simple in that everyone knows that, should the unfortunate happen, you need to be able to have the resources to replace items that are damaged, to pay medical bills or to compensate others for their damaged property. Insurance provides those resources that, at Farmers, we refer to as "getting you back where you belong." Yet it is a difficult concept in that there is no tangible product that is sold, except for a promise to indemnify should the unfortunate happen.

The principle of insurance is to exchange an unknown (uncertainty about what may happen in the future) for a known (an insurance premium paid in advance, as a fee for transferring that uncertainty to someone else). A person doesn't know, for example, whether or not he or she will get into an automobile accident, how much it's going to cost to repair the vehicle, to pay medical bills or how much somebody may sue for. That person doesn't know what the financial consequences of an accident would be, but, by having insurance, they would know that they would be able to meet their obligations up to the limit of insurance they buy. The customer exchanges payment for two very important intangibles, peace of mind and the insurance company promise to pay should an unfortunate incident occur. Insurance provides a degree of certainty in the lives of people or businesses. Of course, insurance isn't limited to automobiles. There's homeowner's insurance, life insurance and business insurance, among others.

When the impact of insurance in our society is considered, a person can easily realize how important it is. Without the availability of insurance, lenders would be reluctant or unable to loan money for automobiles or homes. Most buildings couldn't be built, and businesses couldn't get started because most *require* insurance or bonds in order to begin the construction process. Even the workers need to be insured, in case of injury on the job.

Without insurance to back major pieces of the economy—for example, to provide insurance on airplanes and on the lives of people who fly in them or, in our personal lives, to insure our homes, autos or small businesses—the modern economy couldn't function. The unknown liabilities are so great that they couldn't be factored into any plan.

And then there's the financial contributions the insurance industry makes to keep our great nation operating. In 2003 alone, the insurance industry paid over $10 billion in federal income taxes, invested $645 billion in bonds that support communities we serve and another $187 billion in investments in other companies and enterprises.

Providing the opportunity for the American economy to function, funding the mechanics of society through the taxes we pay and investing in the growth of American business is why insurance is so important for keeping the entire free enterprise system working.

Differentiators Among Insurance Companies

Insurance companies come in all shapes and sizes and in a number of different configurations.

They can be segmented based on different lines of business served. For example, some companies specialize in personal lines, which deal with the activities and property of families and small businesses. Other companies focus on small commercial businesses or huge global corporations. Some are life insurance-focused, while others provide medical insurance. The list goes on and on. Because there are so many lines of insurance, a company can be differentiated simply by saying, "We are going to operate within one of those segments," or it can choose to be a multi-line company and cover many of those segments.

That's just one dimension of how insurance companies differ. Another is by its form of distribution. Some companies sell strictly what we call "1-800 low-cost insurance." There are some that sell on the Internet. Some companies use affinity-based distribution, marketing to groups of people with similar characteristics, such as occupation. Some sell through independent agents and still others sell through exclusive agents that represent only one company, which is the primary distribution system for Farmers. We also use independent agents in some new markets. Finally, some companies use a combination of these various distribution systems.

We have a market segment we've identified that we call "Middle America," average families and small businesses. Of course, other large companies are in this segment too. So, the next step is to differentiate ourselves from these companies in the minds of the consumer. In other words, what do we do best?

A company can also differentiate itself based on price, but we decided that distinguishing ourselves on price alone is not the right way, because people who shop on price alone tend to move from company to company often. So, we differentiate ourselves by emphasizing that our value proposition includes personal, face-to-face service. We rely on trusted professionals, our agents. By providing a one-stop shop for customers, we take care of the vast majority of our customers' insurance needs, making it *easier* for them and reducing a lot of uncertainty in their lives. We help give our customers peace of mind so they can live their lives without worrying about all the things they've worked so hard to acquire.

In today's society, people value quality of life. Farmers helps provide some of that value. With dedicated insurance agents serving them, our customers have less worry about gaps in their coverage. Things are taken care of by one company and one agent. The agent is a trusted professional who helps the customer make decisions concerning his or her insurance needs. The Farmers customer does not have to go -it-alone as many Internet and "1-800" customers have found that they have had to do.

Companies can also differentiate on many factors besides lines of business, types of products, form(s) of distribution, cost and service. In the United States, there are companies that specialize in certain geographic areas. Some are just single-state or regional operations. And there are companies that operate under a specific legal structure. For example, there are stock companies, which are owned and operated by shareholders; there are mutual companies, which are owned and operated by policyholders; and then there are reciprocal exchanges, which are owned by policyholders and managed by an external attorney-in-fact.

Determining Price

One interesting aspect of insurance compared to other industries is pricing. Unlike other industries in which there is a cost of manufacturing the product based on things like material and labor, the insurance industry must price a product without knowing its cost at the time of the sale. That is a wide range that can be predicted only through calculations based upon the experience of like people engaged in like activities over a period of time. The insurance industry relies on the "law of large numbers" and has actuaries and statisticians conduct analyses on past performance to help predict the future. For example, that's why long-distance commuters have different prices for their auto insurance than those drivers who just travel around their town. They drive many more miles per year, increasing the chances of them getting into an accident. We price for the probability of losses, size of losses and the legal environment for something that may not happen for years.

The fact is, some years the insurance industry makes money, and some years it loses money, primarily because it is such a volatile and unpredictable environment.

Predicting the future isn't easy. It's hard. We draw on as many resources as possible. You have to understand the impact of today's variables on tomorrow's world. In the United States market compared to other parts of the world, we have many more variables to take into account.

We don't know what the economy will be doing in the future, but we can make projections based on what we know has happened in the past. For example, historically, the price of gasoline impacts the ultimate number of automobile accidents because the more people have to pay for gasoline the fewer miles they drive. We have to understand how and why these things happen. Whether people are going to buy a lot of new vehicles is dependent upon what employment rates are. If they don't buy new vehicles, the average value of the vehicles on the road is affected, and we build that into our price. If, on the other hand, everyone is trading in their old vehicles for new, more costly ones, we must take that into account. Then we get into calculating the impact of design features, such as safety enhancements. In fact, the safety features put into vehicles by manufacturers in the last couple of years are increasing the cost of repairing vehicles. They have a potential for reducing injury, but the vehicle repair cost is substantially more. We have to consider all of these factors.

We must understand other economic factors, such as the growth in new housing starts that influence the cost of things. If there are going to be a lot of new homes, we may have to invest dollars in preparing for growth spurts in certain geographic areas and allocate capital so we can grow that business. To capitalize on such opportunities, we have to anticipate what the economy is going to do.

Government regulation makes the United States marketplace a little more challenging. First, insurance is probably one of the most regulated industries in the United States. And second, insurance is regulated independently in each of the fifty states, unlike banking, which has a federal regulator. Not only does each state have its own regulatory scheme, every state has its own regulators, which includes the personalities of fifty sets of people with their own focuses and biases on particular issues. So, from a regulatory standpoint, anything can happen from "A" to "Z". To complicate matters even further, each state has its own premium tax laws.

Then there's legislative activity in any given state. We engage in public policy debate because state legislatures make decisions that could fundamentally and dramatically increase the cost of insurance.

We also have to monitor the legal system. We know there is a significant amount of case history, which we follow. The big risk lies in accurately predicting what they'll decide *next*, because the courts continue to surprise us in a number of ways, even on cases involving seemingly straightforward decisions. That uncertainty also affects the cost of insurance.

It's a complex environment. At Farmers, we frequently reassess all these issues and try to decide how much weight to assign each. Then we build a model to project what the future might be. That is not done just once a year, but on a regular basis, because all the pieces are in constant motion.

Planning for Cash from Policies

It's important to understand what is paid for out of every premium dollar the insurance industry collects. The vast majority goes to paying claims and then for salaries, commissions and overhead. The rest, and sometimes that's a small margin, is profit.

Many people are unaware of the fact that insurance premiums cannot immediately be counted as earnings by the company that collects them. Insurance regulation requires that you actually earn the premium one day at a time. So, on an annual policy, we do not earn 100 percent of the premium on the first day, but $1/365^{th}$ of it. That tiny fraction, rather than the whole sum, is all that's available to pay claims and expenses on day one, even though we may be liable for millions of dollars worth of exposure to loss from the moment the policy becomes effective.

One of the things we can do while we're holding the money is to invest it. Here again, insurance regulation imposes restrictions on what kinds of investments are permissible and in what proportions. Regulators also take investment returns into account in determining that the rates insurers charge are adequate but not excessive. In addition, regulators, over time, have demanded that some benefit must be realized by policyholders because you are holding this money (the premium paid but not yet earned) and making money on it. We have it, but we don't have all of it until the end of the policy's period.

But returns are not guaranteed. Usually we make money, but sometimes we don't. For instance, we may earn a low return on fixed rate investments, while claims inflation is two or three times more than anticipated. In that situation, the investment income doesn't make up the shortfall.

Another reason we invest the money while we are "holding" it is to increase our ability to write more business and to deliver on our promise to be there when our customers need us, in other words, to settle claims. We have to have more money in our bank account than is needed to pay known claims and expenses. These extra funds are called "surplus." Regulators require that insurance companies have a sufficient amount of money on hand at all times to pay for potential claims, plus a sizeable cushion for contingencies. Therefore, for every dollar you are willing to accept from a customer, you have to have a certain amount of money already sitting in your bank account that is readily available to pay claims in the future. We do everything we can to enhance the surplus through investment.

Determining the Premium

Premium volume depends on the line of business and the type of coverage. Rates also vary widely from company to company, since the industry is highly competitive and because setting them is subject to anti-trust laws that prohibit insurers from even discussing the rates they plan to charge.

Every company takes its own strategic approach as to how it is going to set rates. That is one of the ways companies can differentiate themselves.

Rates are usually determined by trying to do two things: first, evaluate the risk, and second, anticipate what the ultimate claims might be, so you'll know what the losses may be. Then you have to evaluate the individual customer to determine the probability of that customer having a claim. You might take a look at how many years the customer has been driving. Do they drive their car to work every day? You might look at their driving record. Do they have any speeding tickets? Accidents? How many other people in the household will be using the car? Do they have any young drivers? How is the vehicle used? Is it driven to work every day or used in employment? How far is it driven? Is it parked in safe places and parked in a garage at night? Any of these factors may increase the chances of a loss. These are just some of the things that are considered.

We gather as many facts as we legally can in forming a picture of the potential risk to help us analyze the exposure and assign a value to it. That value has to be based on fact. We then take the data of similar risks and try to determine a cost. In this process, we must also consider each state's individual pricing regulations.

We have extensive computer systems that aggregate an enormous amount of data on claims, claims payments, our own customers and even demographics of the general population. We use the data to build our pricing model. In some lines of insurance, particularly private passenger auto and homeowners, risk-scoring methods that take factors such as personal responsibility into account have recently come into wide usage. These factors can often help build a better picture of the individual's attributes and the true nature of the risk that he or she present. A more accurate risk profile enables us to rate each risk more fairly. Although we use large groups of similar risks to set rates, our goal is to determine and charge the most accurate rate for the *individual* risk profile.

In the old days, companies used broad categories to classify risk, with few real distinctions between the categories or the prices charged for the exposure. By employing more sophisticated modeling techniques in both auto and homeowners insurance, we are trying to charge the right rate for the right risk. In fact, in our extremely competitive market, this is a must—a core competency.

Finding New Customers

Marketing is essential to gaining new customers. Marketing begins with reputation. You have to have a value system upon which your credibility in the marketplace is based.

Effective marketing includes building a positive image in the community. In our organization, we believe we have to be good citizens in the states, cities and communities in which we sell insurance. We want to be a part of the community. That's why we support such organizations as the Insurance Institute for Highway Safety, which is dedicated to reducing deaths, injuries and property damage on the nation's highways. We, like other insurance companies, fund the organization so it can research automobile safety and educate people on such issues as teen driving safety, airbag safety, child safety seats and many others.

We also have to make sure our story is told in the media. We want to make sure we are engaged, not just in getting people to buy insurance, but also in understanding the role of insurance and in communicating important insurance issues. Therefore, we participate in numerous associations that offer practical information. One such organization is The Insurance Information Institute. It is a source for information about insurance for the media and a variety of other users.

Beyond these efforts, it's important to enhance the brand. We operate our business on the principle, based on research, that people want their lives restored to order following a loss. We know that some companies may sell insurance at a lower rate, but, in the back of people's minds, what they really want is comfort and peace of mind so that should something happen, there will be someone there to help take care of them. We built our brand promise — Farmers. Gets You Back Where You Belong — around that commitment. And it's not only in our advertising, direct mail, and marketing material; it's in how we act day-in, day-out with those who, unfortunately, are facing losses.

A major part of our marketing is done through our agents. Our primary distribution system is what we refer to as "The Farmers Agent." These are independent contractors who exclusively offer our product and service our customers. They operate their own agencies, live in the communities where they do business, are moms and dads and participate in community activities, such as the PTA and youth soccer. They *live* our brand. They are known and respected in the community, and, at the same time, they sell insurance and take care of customers.

Today, people's mailboxes are filled with direct mail offers selling insurance at lower rates. Even newspapers carry these stuffers, to say nothing of all of the "spam" that comes across the Internet. But having a marketing strategy is much more than offering a rate or how many impressions you can make through your advertising. It is being able to get into the community and mean something to it. When you buy insurance, you need a company that's going to be there if, in fact, you are in an automobile accident, your home is damaged or you suffer a death in the family. You have to have someone who will deliver in your time of need. Farmers works hard to build that kind of credibility, to earn that kind of trust.

Facing and Hedging Risks

Each line of insurance coverage has a different risk profile. An industry-wide practice, followed in our own organization, is to have a professional risk-management function that does an analysis called a total risk profile. We look at all of the trends and try to determine what the issues are, then build a specific action plan for mitigating the most significant risks. Some can't be mitigated, and you have to decide to either suspend that line of business or to write an insurance contract that limits your exposure. Or you can pay someone else to assume the risk.

Insurance written by one insurer that limits the exposure of another is known as reinsurance. One example of how an insurance company uses reinsurance to mitigate risk is to decrease exposure to major catastrophic events. No area of the country is immune from some major weather exposure, whether it is hurricanes, tornadoes, hailstorms or something else. Usually these storms happen in concentrated areas with the possibility of near-universal destruction in that area. If an insurance company was to insure numerous homes or cars in an area, and that area was heavily damaged, the insurance company could be facing financial hardship. For a price, the company can transfer ("reinsure") a portion of that exposure to another company. In this example, buying reinsurance helps the insurance company mitigate its exposure to large catastrophic events and the resulting financial impact in the same fashion as buying insurance helps an individual protect him or herself from the economic consequences of damage to personal property.

Purchasing reinsurance is just one of many potential strategies companies can use to avoid or mitigate the risks confronting their businesses. Well-run companies, regardless of the industry, have a similar process of identifying, evaluating and mitigating risks.

Selecting the Good Risks

Insurance companies make business choices in selecting *individual* risks and in selecting the *overall* amount of risk they're comfortable with. To "discriminate" is to recognize differences, such as when an individual has a limited amount of money to spend, and they must choose (discriminate) between two investments. Just as that person would review all of the objective merits that make one investment better than another, an insurance company, before choosing to invest (take a risk), makes choices in their underwriting selection process. Indeed, any process of selection requires us to discriminate, to recognize differences between options and to make choices. The process of risk selection in the insurance business works the same way.

Insurance regulation permits companies to discriminate, as long as they do not do so unfairly. There must be a causal relationship between the existence of a risk's characteristics and the insurer's choice not to insure it or to charge for the trait's existence. For example, we couldn't say we choose not to insure people who wear plaid clothing just because we don't like plaid clothing or because we simply *believe* that people who wear plaid clothing are poor risks. That might be viewed as being *unfairly* discriminatory. However, if we could demonstrate that there is a causal relationship between plaid clothing and loss frequency/severity, we could use it to determine eligibility or pricing for people who wear plaid. This is why insurers are allowed to consider prior driving citations to determine rate and eligibility for coverage; we have proven that the occurrence of the citations affect future loss frequency.

Some insurance companies believe that virtually all risks are insurable at the right price. They believe that it is simply a matter of identifying the appropriate rate for the specific risk presented and whether the person is willing to pay that price. There are insurance companies in the United

States, for example, that specialize just in "high risk" drivers, who must pay higher prices than the average-risk driver to get insurance. If they are willing and able to pay the price the company has established for the higher risk they present, then the company is willing to insure them.

Different insurers also choose the level of *overall* risk and exposure they are comfortable with, and that is how they choose to allot capital, i.e. invest in their business. Again, this is much like how an individual chooses to invest personal income. Insurers (in fact, all businesses) make choices where to allot capital.

The important message here, regarding selecting good risks, is that insurance companies use objective, quantifiable data to select and price risks. You need to prove that the price you are charging is fair and based upon fact and that your choices in selecting those risks meet the same criteria.

Challenging Aspects in the Insurance Business

Everything in our industry is challenging.

It is a dynamic industry, and you can't be asleep at the switch. You have to spot the newest trends before they hit the marketplace. If you don't, another company will get the business and you won't, and/or it will impact what you will pay in claims because you may not be collecting enough premiums to pay for them.

The most frustrating part, obviously, is trying to predict what may happen in a rapidly changing legislative, regulatory and judicial environment. We, as individuals, like to have some degree of certainty so we can make decisions. But there are so many moving parts in the insurance industry that it sometimes becomes challenging to manage all the variables outside your span of control.

There are a lot of resources available to help executives, including insurance publications and insurance associations. In fact, there are a number of institutes that do unique research on particular issues. I am the vice chairman of the CEO Roundtable, which is comprised of executives of the top fifteen insurance companies in the United States. The CEO Roundtable's main function is to look at public policy issues. We have a responsibility to our policyholders, our shareholders and to our employees to make sure we are up-to-date on the issues that affect them and that we investigate and discuss public policy issues. Does that mean we have all the answers? No. But it's important to explore the questions to find those answers we can.

Dealing with Customers Amidst Constant Change

We have a responsibility to keep our customers up-to-date on important issues that directly affect them. There are many public, independent sources for doing that, such as the Insurance Information Institute, but we also want to assist customers in understanding insurance issues that might affect them.

In our organization we do three major things, among others:

First, we publish a magazine, "Friendly Exchange," for our customers, which is not an insurance magazine. It is a magazine full of information our customers can use to better their lives, whether it is travel, technology issues, financial information, and it even offers some ways in which they can use insurance and financial services to solve their worries and achieve their dreams. The magazine also serves as a forum, so we can talk about the issues. We think that's important.

Second, we have a responsibility to provide information to our agents, which we do through a variety of publications that we supply to our agents. Or we suggest publications our agents can buy to send to their customers so the customers are kept up-to-date on important issues.

Third, working through our media relations department, we constantly talk to the media about key issues, not just when there is a big lawsuit or when something bad has happened. For example, we recently published a study we commissioned on cities around the nation that have a higher incidence of theft and burglary claims. It helps people when deciding where they want to live. Or, maybe they could get involved with their civic authorities to get them to do a better job of protecting homes.

Doing these things goes back to a basic philosophy that we aren't here just to collect premiums, we also have to participate in the communities in which we work and live.

An Industry of Change

One of the biggest drivers of change in the insurance business is technology. In fact, technology has significantly changed the industry in the last five years, from the lowest level, in terms of how we print and issue policies and send out bills; to a higher level of how we collect and analyze data to better understand what's happening; to perhaps the highest level, which has to do with how we model and do sophisticated pricing. All of these are driven by technology today.

The second biggest driver is the fact that consumers are changing the ways and means by which they are buying insurance.

The last driver of change is the buying habits of consumers. The "baby boomers" are the fastest growing segment of the population. They are gathering wealth at a more rapid pace than any previous generation. They are buying things that were never broadly owned before. Farmers' "baby boomer strategy" was built five years ago when we noticed that baby boomers are buying boats, homes, motorcycles, motor homes, manufactured homes, mobile homes, recreational property and other "toys." We made a decision, based on the fact that consumers are changing, that we couldn't just offer auto or home policies without being able to cover other things just as expertly. We actually went out and acquired a company to provide us with the capability to provide insurance for these types of possessions.

In managing change, insurance companies have to look at the leading indicators. We have to do things based on fact for rating, risk selection and things of that nature. But the trouble with fact is that it is always old news. It means we've already had a claim submitted. A year has already gone by, or two or three. A lot of what we get from a financial standpoint is like looking through the rear window of a car while driving ahead. That's why we need to always be paying attention to leading indicators. They let us know that we are focused on the road ahead.

Potential Changes

There are a lot of issues being discussed that are quite controversial. Because they are controversial, you may not know whether they are entirely good or bad until they actually happen.

One controversial issue is to try to resolve the question of state-by-state regulation versus centralized federal oversight. It is an important topic for three reasons:

First, regulation is cumbersome in its current state-by-state form. Companies like ours cope very well and are perfectly willing to work with it, but a lot of insurance companies have products that compete with banks, investment companies and global insurers that may involve other types of regulators. They feel that, as a result, the playing field is not level.

Second, the cost of managing regulation on a state-by-state basis can be significant. Individual state-knowledgeable staffs are needed to keep up on all the unique state laws and rules. And then you have to file and publish separate rates, marketing data and everything else. These are all expenses we have to pass on to the consumer.

Third, as proposed laws are debated in Washington, D.C., the financial services industry generally has an advantage over insurance companies. Having just one regulator to deal with, the financial services industry can concentrate their efforts and speak with a louder voice in getting appropriate bills or laws passed. Whereas when a global, federal regulator does not represent you, it makes it more difficult to get commonality in an approach toward certain issues. This is something that's constantly discussed.

The House and Senate have taken this issue under consideration, but they are leaning more towards setting some type of national standards, rather than establishing a federal regulator. But even that would change the industry for the better. Companies could be quicker to market with products and pricing changes, quicker to market in licensing agents across state lines and quicker to become new entrants to markets to provide greater capacity for writing new business. There are a lot of benefits that may come from it, but it's certainly a hot issue.

Another issue that would change the face of the industry is class-action-lawsuit reform. I can't speak for others, but I believe that people have the right to file lawsuits, the right to have their cases heard and the right to be appropriately compensated for damages if they have been wronged. However, the growth in class action litigation has created a great dilemma because of the huge expense associated with it versus the benefit to the consumer. The issue is the growing cost of indemnification, which is ultimately passed on to the consumer in higher rates. The industry believes people must have the right to bring class actions, but there needs to be a little more structure and process to ensure that it is fair and not financially burdensome to the consumer. It's a growing problem, not just for the insurance industry, but also for all commerce. The cost is being passed on to the consumers through the prices of cars, refrigerators and other commodities and services as businesses must pay higher rates for insurance to cover these losses.

Effects of Terrorism

The industry has been impacted to some degree by the terrorist attacks of September 11, 2001. The threat of renewed attacks is something on the list of things that keeps us up at night. It is a very real worry, and we have to be thinking about it. It has changed the way a lot of companies look at aggregation of risk (how much of what type of business is concentrated where). There is no way to completely mitigate risk in this case because nobody knows when the next terrorist attack will be or in what form it would take.

It is challenging when we try to figure out "what ifs," but all insurance companies must do this. In the wake of 9/11, Congress approved a federal terror risk insurance-type program as a backstop to the industry. Legislation to extend the Terrorism Risk Insurance Act has just come before Congress. It is a backstop that will probably never be used by the insurance industry unless there is a huge financial catastrophe as a result of a major attack. But it affords some comfort that the industry would not go bankrupt as the result of another major terrorist attack. If the Act is not renewed or replaced by something else, a lot of large commercial lines companies will be the first to feel the impact. The question, from the insurance industry perspective, is would you want to insure large office buildings and provide workers' compensation to employees where you have thousands of people working in the same building or location? Do you want to have a high concentration of risk in a geographic part of any city where, if something goes wrong, there would be a substantial impact?

Since 9/11, the group life reinsurance companies have been concerned about the effects of a major terrorist attack. It's a public policy issue, as, in many cases, group life insurance is the only life insurance coverage that a worker might have. Life re-insurers are urging Congress to pass legislation that would provide a financial safety back-up if a major terrorist strike hits the United States.

As realists, we think it may be impossible to protect us forever from everything. But 9/11 has made us much more alert to the issues. Such risks weren't high on the probability list before 9/11, but once the unthinkable happened, these risks moved up immediately, and we all had to factor them in. Unfortunately, that is the world that we live in today, a different world, fraught with new risks. Yet, we are not discouraged as we look to the future. After all, managing risk is our business.

Conclusion

Insurance is complex, from the various types of companies, to the multitude of products and services, to the ways in which the products are sold and to the way prices are established. That's because of its very nature of dealing with an intangible product with unknown future costs. But, it's a much needed industry, providing the underpinnings of our society and opportunities for the very economy in which it operates to function and grow. Farmers is one of the major "players" in the American marketplace and is proud of its contributions to helping people to achieve their dreams and to get people back to where they belong should an unfortunate incident occur. We are very proud of what we do and our place in society.

Mr. Feinstein joined Farmers in 1970 as a Liability Claims Representative in the Los Angeles Regional Office. After serving in several regional offices throughout the country, he was promoted to Regional Claims Manager for the Pocatello, Idaho Regional Office in 1980 and held a similar position in the Pleasanton, Calif. Regional Office. In 1984 he became Regional Sales Manager in Pleasanton; he returned to the Home Office in January 1986 as Director of Sales Support in the marketing department.

Mr. Feinstein was assigned to the Executive Training Program in January 1988. He was appointed Assistant Vice President of Farmers Group, Inc. and named Regional Manager of the Los Angeles Regional Office in 1988. Mr. Feinstein served in this capacity until transferring to Home Office in November 1989 as Vice President of Marketing. In January 1993 he was appointed Senior Vice President of Special Projects. Mr. Feinstein was appointed Senior Vice President of Property and Casualty Staff, on October 1, 1993, during this time he also held the position of Chief Information Officer. On January 1, 1995, he was promoted to President and Chief Operating Officer. He was elected to the board of directors February 5, 1995. Effective January 1, 1997, Mr. Feinstein was elected President and Chief Executive Officer. On November 10, 1997 he was also assigned as a Member of the Group Executive Committee – Zurich Financial Services. Mr. Feinstein's current assignment became effective July 1, 2004.

Mr. Feinstein received a bachelor of science from California State University at Los Angeles. He also received his Chartered Property and Casualty Underwriter (CPCU), Chartered Life Underwriter (CLU), Graduate in Claims Administration (GCA), and Associate in Claims (AIC) designations. He earned the Insurance Institute of America (IIA) general insurance certificate, as well.

Mr. Feinstein was born in Cleveland, Ohio and now resides with his wife, Naomi, in Thousands Oaks, California. They have two children.

The Business of Insuring Business

Mark E. Watson

President & Chief Executive Officer
Argonaut Group, Inc.

Introduction

All businesses face risk. Every company, large and small, faces an array of physical and financial dangers. It is impossible to completely eliminate risks, but it is possible to greatly reduce the financial impacts. My organization, the companies of Argonaut Group, provides financial protection for businesses through an array of insurance products and risk management services.

The insurance needs of a business are typically more complex than the insurance needs of an average person. These commercial risks are assessed based upon the type of business, the nature of the operations, the size of the company and a variety of other factors. In this way, a business is able to partner with its insurer to identify and then develop strategies to manage many of the physical and legal risks inherent in running a company.

Tactics used to measure risk depend on the type of risk. Different tools allow insurance companies to evaluate every exposure they insure. If a client is in the technology industry, for example, he or she may look at how much time an employee spends typing on his or her computer each day, as one of the biggest claims in that industry is carpel tunnel syndrome. If the client is a city or town, as another example, it may be more interested in the number of police cars or the number of miles of road in a particular town or county.

Insurance leverages a simple principle. When a business buys an insurance policy, its goal is to spread the risk with a lot of other policyholders. The presumption is that some of these businesses will have a claim (or claims), but many of them will not. Since none of us have a crystal ball, which might better predict who will have a claim, business can protect their balance sheets by sharing risk. They pool together the premiums of the group to pay for the losses of those few. Sophisticated models and experience help insurance companies predict the frequency and severity of losses within a particular industry or class of business.

Small businesses require different approaches to risk management than larger companies. In a small company, the average premium may be a few hundred to a few thousand dollars per year, and the chances of having a claim may be slim. For large companies, the question is not will there be a loss in any one year, but how many losses will there be in that year and how severe will those losses be? With proper risk management tools, their balance sheets may face tremendous exposure. That's where we come in.

Larger companies engage in a variety of efforts to minimize these losses through a variety of methods. These include safety engineering, quality control, back to work programs for injured employees, customer and employee education and improvements in their facilities. In each case our goal is to first identify the risk and then use our risk management tools to eliminate risk of claims from occurring, through safety programs, or mitigate losses once a risk has occurred.

Basic Operations of an Insurance Company

Setting Premiums

The basic principles of insurance are rather straightforward; the operations necessary to achieve them are fairly complex. These complex operations are used to achieve the cornerstones of the insurance industry: setting appropriate premiums, managing capital efficiently, underwriting risks with discipline and the process of evaluating and paying claims.

Premiums are primarily determined by the customer's industry. Insurance companies have data- bases that take into consideration the different risk characteristics at a general level. The insurer asks a series of underwriting questions to try and better understand the exact risk profile of the customer. Insurers are interested in such things as the customer's revenue, the number of employees and the type of business; all of these questions are geared toward determining the exposure level.

Once that process is complete, the insurer looks at the loss history of the insured. Some companies may not have had any losses, and some may have had a lot. The number (frequency) and size (severity) of losses will factor into the final cost for the insurance. The insurer typically works with an independent insurance agent or insurance broker. These specially-trained and licensed salespeople will then present a quote to the customer. An insurance quote includes the price and the terms and conditions of the policy. Agents and Brokers also work with clients to evaluate and recommend adequate amounts of insurance and appropriate risk management services. The agent or broker works with the insurance company and the client to bind the coverage (the policy) and initiate the safety management and loss control services required.

The Role of the Underwriter

To determine the exact risk profile of a customer, the underwriter evaluates responses to a series of questions. These questions examine the customer's revenue, the number of employees and their type of business, all of these geared toward determining the magnitude and level of risk exposure. A large repository of data and models and experience provide underwriters with a holistic view of the business to be insured. They take into consideration the number of claims or losses the specific business has experienced and compare that to the industry. Some businesses experience a great number of losses, while others may see none. The underwriter relies on his or her expertise to bring all of this together.

The underwriter's role is to accept or reject a risk. If the underwriter agrees to issue a policy, he or she will provide a detailed price that is specific to that risk and the policy being requested. An agent or broker, representing the insurer, will present a detailed quote to the customer. The quote contains information about the price, the specific terms and conditions, the specific exposure insured and the level of safety and loss control services being offered.

Evaluating Claims

The claims process begins after a loss occurs. Often a business will receive a "notice of loss" or injury from a third party (customer, vendor, etc.). Other times, a claim is filed when an accident involves one of its employees. Sometimes, a claim is initiated because there is a reasonable belief that a recent event will result in a loss sometime in the future. As soon as an accident or event occurs, the business alerts the insurance company. The insurance company (and policyholder) may hear about a claim for the first time because the policyholder (business) receives notice that they are being sued.

No matter how the claim is initiated, the insurance company will investigate the claim, determine whether the claim is covered under one or more policies held by the client, how the loss occurred, who is responsible and the amount of financial loss that resulted. The investigation is performed by a specially trained insurance adjustor. That person is responsible for the determination of coverage, investigation of facts and payments that will be made. Insurance companies have a legal duty to thoroughly investigate all claims. The results of these investigations determine the amount of money that the insurance company must set aside (reserve) to pay the claim. The monies reserved for claims are strictly regulated and used solely for that purpose.

The process can be complicated. And making it more challenging is the reality that it can sometimes take days, weeks, months or even years after an accident occurs before a claim is actually filed. The complex nature and differences among businesses have led to a vast array of insurance policies with differing language, covering differing risks and for a variety of time periods. Whether a claim is paid by the insurer ultimately depends upon the language in the policy.

Who is Argonaut?

Argonaut Group, Inc. is a national specialty underwriter. Through our family of companies, we operate in four distinct segments of the commercial insurance market, the largest of which is our excess and surplus lines business. Today, the excess and surplus market is one of the fastest growing parts of the insurance industry and comprises our largest segment. As businesses become more complex, so do the risks associated with them. The second-largest piece of the group would be our risk-management business, where we're providing casualty solutions to larger businesses throughout the US. These are larger businesses that are interested in managing their risk and are looking for insurance partners to help them do that. Again, for these businesses, it's not a question of will they have a claim, but how many will they have, and what can we do to manage that risk.

What has grown into the third-largest segment of our company on a pro forma basis is our public entity business, which is now positioned to make us the second-largest national underwriter of small to medium-size public entities in the US. Our fourth segment, which we refer to as "specialty commercial," provides package policies to small businesses in specific industries, this segment has also grown through the recent renewal rights acquisition of Grocers Insurance, America's leading independent insurer of food merchants. The addition of Grocers Insurance to the specialty commercial segment establishes Argonaut as the leading insurance provider for independent grocery stores.

There are a number of different underwriting organizations within the Argonaut group, and many of them are known by another name. These various operating subsidiaries differentiate the products and services that they deliver from one part of the group to another. This product strategy allows the companies within Argonaut Group to maintain their individual focuses while leveraging the capital strength and company brand that the Argonaut Group provides.

Differentiating One Insurance Company from Another

At Argonaut, we believe that our job isn't just to sell insurance policies. It is also about helping businesses manage their risks. We believe that a number of things differentiate insurance companies from each other, but the most important is service. Service can be seen during the claims process, after a loss occurs, but it also comes *before* the loss. The best safety and loss control services are those that prevent a loss from occurring. These services may differ vastly from one insurance company to another. The premier insurance companies partner with their agents and business clients to prevent losses from ever happening, identifying technologies, tools and techniques that results in fewer losses and fewer claims. This keeps the insurance costs down for everyone.

Pricing also differentiates companies. Some companies try to play the commodity game. They write a large volume of policies, assuming that economies of scale and rapid processing capabilities will lower overhead and, therefore, allow them to offer a lower price. Other insurers focus on the quality of those that they insure (through specialized underwriting) rather than volume of customers or expediency alone. They seek to create greater value through better practices. In this way, price alone is often a misleading method of selecting an insurer. The old adage of "you get what you pay for" is certainly true in our industry. You can always find a less expensive alternative, but then you have to ask yourself if the insurance company understands your business or if they will be there when it's time to pay a claim. Argonaut Group deploys capital and other resources to deliver superior value and superior service.

Financial stability is another differentiator, because some companies are better capitalized than others. When you are buying insurance for exposures that may take years to show up and take years before they will be paid, you want to make certain your insurance company is going to be around. Conversely, when you have a widespread catastrophe like fires, earthquakes or floods, it is important that your insurance company have the financial capital to pay the resulting claims.

Over the last fifty years, some insurers have distinguished themselves by developing a number of innovative products and services that have put them on the front end of providing risk management tools to customers. One tool developed by Argonaut is called S.T.A.R.T. (Supervisor Training in Accident Reduction Techniques). This is an accountability-based, safety management seminar for managers and supervisors of the businesses we insure. We developed this program to provide customers with modern safety management concepts; methods that have proven successful in dramatically reducing accident costs.

Shopping for an Insurance Company

Selecting an insurer that best fits the needs of your business can be a daunting task. There are three basic areas that you should consider in making your selection. First, track the company's financial results to assess its stability in the marketplace and financial solvency. Second, assess the company's policy retention rate over the past two years; this gives you a sense of overall customer satisfaction. Third, review its underwriting and claims handling processes. How are claims reported?

To track financial results, pay attention to new products and initiatives that are coming out of the company. What is its turnover rate? How many accounts actually stay with the company from one year to the next? How do its rates fluctuate both up and down relative to changes or anticipated changes and exposure going forward?

Challenges in the Industry

Regulatory Challenges

The insurance industry differs from most in the volume and segmentation of government regulation. The industry is regulated by each state's legal and legislative environments, with federal oversight. Insurance regulations can and do vary from state to state and affect many insurance activities. Regulation affects producer (insurance agent) licensing, how claims are processed and paid and the wording of insurance policies. In addition, the judicial system in each state interprets and rules upon the language in insurance contracts, often requiring clarification and alteration of the policies, practices and pricing.

Because insurance is a regulated industry, it takes more time to react to the marketplace. Whenever insurers want to change what they charge or the types of coverage they provide, they have to go back to the state regulators to get permission. Imagine if this requirement were placed on your industry. Should the makers of breakfast cereal acquire government approval of pricing? What about toothpaste or your local drive-through restaurant? What role should the government play in pricing?

Financial Challenges

Unlike most other businesses, insurance companies don't know the real costs of the products they sell at the time they sell them. It may be many years after the policy is sold that the true costs are known. Managing risk is something that insurance companies must practice themselves. Over time, insurers accrue what they think their losses are going to be, based upon past experience and sophisticated actuarial modeling. This is especially important in workers compensation and general liability insurance.

General liability policies can be open ended for a long time. Cases involving asbestos exposure are a good example of why companies need this insurance. Many companies are still filing for bankruptcy because of the law suits that have been brought against them. Most of the monies being paid for asbestos related injuries are coming from claims made against the insurance policies written thirty plus years ago. So, it is easy to see that insurers are issuing policies today with limited knowledge of what exposures they may be covering in the future. And future judicial and legislative actions may even amend what is covered by the policies written today as some unexpected loss appears in future years.

The time between when a policy is issued, the premium is paid and the claims are paid out could constitute a number of years. Insurance companies have the opportunity to make some money on the held cash, or "the float," by investing it. It is not an open-ended investment opportunity. There are regulations that limit the types of investments. The majority of the money is invested in bonds and some publicly-held large stocks. The Argonaut Insurance Group prefers a conservative investment portfolio where the security offsets the consistency of the yield on the investment. While there is a chance to make some money on the float until it is paid out in claims, it should not drive the business or the financial results of the company. Underwriting results, not the ability to make returns on investments, determines the success of the insurer.

Looking Ahead

In the future, our industry must move to take more costs out of the operating structure. There must also be more transparency relative to the operations of insurance companies, as well as more uniformity among the states when it comes to regulation.

In order for us to provide the best products and services, we must be able to move more quickly as our customer's needs change. Regulators need to get more comfortable with the idea that capital markets actually work. Pricing trends do reflect the cost of risk being assumed by an insurer. If someone is charging too high of a price, it is only a matter of time before one or more of the hundreds or thousands of companies in a particular marketplace come back in with better pricing. A market economy assures everyone of competitive pricing and quality products.

Mr. Watson is president and chief executive officer of Argonaut Group Inc., a $3 billion property and casualty insurance group. Argonaut is a national *specialty underwriter, writing in four major segments of the market: excess and surplus, risk management, specialty commercial and public entity.*

Prior to joining Argonaut, Mr. Watson was a founding partner of Aquila Capital Partners, a Texas based venture capital firm focused on technology and life science related companies. Before founding Aquila, Mr. Watson was an executive vice president and member of the board of directors of Titan Holding, Inc., a NYSE listed property and casualty insurance group from 1992 until its acquisition in 1998 by USF&G Corporation. From 1989 to 1991, he was an associate attorney with Kroll & Tract, a New York law firm focusing on international financial services clientele.

Mr. Watson graduated with a B.B.A. from Southern Methodist University and a J.D. from the University of Texas, School of Law. While in school, Mr. Watson was a member of the SMU sailing team and ice hockey team, as well as being elected to the SMU Student Senate.

Mr. Watson is an avid climber and sailor having climbed on several continents.

Property/Casualty Insurance: A Business of Risk & Reward

Constantine "Dinos" Iordanou
President & Chief Executive Officer
Arch Capital Group Ltd.

The Basics of the Property/Casualty Insurance Business

Risk is everywhere. It touches virtually every facet of the lives of individuals and the operations of enterprise. The insurance industry is in the business of assuming and managing the numerous and diverse risks that impact our world.

Individuals and businesses pay premiums to transfer their risks to insurance companies. By doing so, the insured party purchases the insurer's contractual promise that if a certain adverse event occurs, the insurer will pay, enabling the insured to protect assets from the financial impact of the event, or at least lessen the resulting financial burden. These adverse events can range from a fire that destroys a family's home, to a liability lawsuit that forces a corporation to pay hefty legal defense fees, settlements or judgments, to medical expenses incurred by an employee who is injured on the job.

Underwriters at insurance companies specialize in assessing the risks confronting people and businesses around the world. These professionals also determine the proper amount of premium the insurer should charge to assume a risk, based on the size of the risk, the terms and conditions to be put forth in the insurance contract and the likelihood that a claim will occur.

An insurance company typically invests the premiums it collects so that its money grows, ensuring its financial ability to pay claims and fulfill its promise to insureds while maintaining a profitable business. Profits come to insurance companies primarily in two ways: underwriting profits, which are monies left over from premiums collected after operating expenses and claims are paid, and investment income, which is the income an insurer generates from investing its capital and the loss reserves maintained on its balance sheet to pay losses.

Major Insurance Industry Players

The two major sectors of the property/casualty insurance business, Personal Lines and Commercial Lines, are dominated by different industry leaders. Personal lines insurance companies predominately write homeowners and auto liability insurance for individuals. They sell policies directly to consumers or through agents and brokers. Dominant companies in this sector include State Farm Insurance, Allstate, Farmers Insurance, Nationwide, Progressive and GEICO.

Commercial lines insurers underwrite property, casualty (or liability) insurance for businesses. They insure commercial enterprises of all types, protecting everything from office buildings, hotels and manufacturing facilities, to warehouses, airlines and trucking companies. Commercial insurance companies typically sell policies through agent or broker intermediaries. Leading companies in this sector include AIG, Zurich, Berkshire Hathaway, Travelers, CNA and Chubb.

The competitive landscape of the insurance industry has been shifting in recent years. Several new players have entered the market, particularly to fill the market's need for replenishing capacity after the catastrophic insured losses from 9/11 forced many insurers out of business. My company, Arch Capital Group Ltd., is one player that responded to this post-9/11 market need. Arch subsidiaries are now among the top thirty insurance companies in the commercial property/casualty segment.

Differentiating One Company from Another

The key elements that differentiate one insurer from another are specialization, underwriting expertise, financial strength, technology and service.

Specialization

An insurer can rarely, if ever, be all things to all people. Hence, specialization is common in the industry. For example, certain personal lines players specialize in policies for high-net-worth individuals and focus on underwriting homes valued in excess of $2 million. Others specialize in insuring lower value residences and the risks of middle-class homeowners.

Commercial lines companies specialize in specific lines of insurance for businesses, such as state-mandated workers' compensation insurance or "specialty" lines, which is a broad category of insurance that encompasses products like professional liability or environmental liability insurance. Many large commercial insurers write multiple lines and devote separate units to particular insurance products (e.g., property, casualty and specialty) and market segments (e.g., small, middle market, national and global accounts).

Expertise

Hand-in-hand with specialization goes expertise. Insurance is essentially a financial services business. The product being manufactured is intangible; a decision to take on a risk according to certain terms and conditions. Financial success rests on the ability of an insurer's underwriters, actuaries and claim professionals to make sound decisions on which risks to assume, at what price. Consequently, the knowledge and skill of an insurance company's professionals is central to the company's ability to make decisions that will sustain profitability and enable it to endure in its chosen lines of business.

Insurance companies are wise to remain focused on areas in which they have significant expertise so that price and risk can be properly assessed on a consistent basis. Occasionally, the displacement of a player from the market tempts some insurers to enter a sector where rates are higher or lower than they should be, and they see potential for short-term gains. Chasing market share in this way is a dangerous strategy, one that has led many insurers into financial trouble.

Technology

Technology can be a powerful competitive advantage for an insurer. Efficient operating processes and systems can drive down costs and provide a wealth of management information. Such management information can provide an insurer with critical insights for evaluating the profitability of various product lines, distribution channels and market niches. Technology can expedite communication and correspondence between the insurer and the insurance purchaser throughout the underwriting process. It can facilitate an underwriter's assessment of a risk by easing access to rich historical data on losses and risk profiles. It can also optimize the most important service a carrier provides, claim service. Online claim reporting alone can add substantial convenience for policyholders and promote a faster claim response from the insurer.

Service

Companies also differentiate themselves in the manner in which they service customers. This is especially true when a claim occurs. As stated earlier, an insurance policy is a contract promising to pay a covered loss if it occurs. That promise must be executed fairly and executed well. And, oftentimes, it requires far more than simply cutting a check in a timely fashion.

Insurers are frequently involved in helping businesses minimize lost revenue by resuming operations as quickly as possible following a loss. Some insurers provide medical case management and rehabilitation services to help an employer return injured workers to productivity swiftly. They may have a duty to defend their insured in certain litigation. On the personal lines side, a consumer may require the insurer's help finding a shop that can repair his or her automobile quickly following an accident claim and funding payment of a rental car while the vehicle remains out of service. Making the claims process smooth and ensuring that a loss causes the least possible disruption to an insured, financially or otherwise, is the central mission of any responsible insurer.

Many insurers also provide pivotal support to help businesses manage risk and prevent or mitigate losses. Such support ranges from engineering services that result in recommendations to create a safer workplace, to training programs that help employers ensure sound labor practices that reduce exposure to employment practices claims. A personal lines insurer might provide services to help high-net-worth individuals with everything from optimizing residential security to safely transporting valuables.

Financial Strength

An insurer must act in good faith to pay promptly all claims that are legally owed under the insurance contract. However, an insurer can only do this if it is financially able. The rapid rise in insurer insolvencies the industry has seen in recent years has left many policyholders with valid claims unpaid. Consequently, the strength of a company's balance sheet and capital base has become a more critical consideration and differentiator than ever before.

Several agencies, including A.M. Best Company, rate the financial strength and claims-paying ability of insurers. The ratings bestowed by these agencies are an important gauge of an insurer's ability to fulfill its financial obligations to policyholders. In this day and age, customers and brokers are also wise to inquire about the history of an insurer, being especially cognizant of "legacy" claims that might be lurking on an insurer's balance sheet from years past. Insurer's with material legacy claims issues have greater demands on their capital than newer insurers with fresh capital.

Pricing Insurance Policies

Properly pricing insurance policies is central to an insurer's ability to pay claims. In order to determine the appropriate rates to charge for various types of businesses and lines of insurance, a company typically analyzes its own detailed statistical claims and exposure experience, as well as data available from outside agencies. While several organizations provide data that is useful in rating insurance policies, the two used most frequently by commercial lines insurers are the Insurance Services Office (ISO), which houses data for numerous commercial lines of insurance, and the National Council of Compensation Insurance (NCCI), which provides data on workers' compensation exposures.

These organizations analyze and disseminate loss cost data based on risk classifications of potential exposure to loss. As a result, these organizations, and individual insurers, project estimates of future losses that will emerge from policies written today.

Industry Challenges

Like all industries, the insurance business faces its share of challenges. Chief among these are ensuring long-term profitability and financial strength, insuring unpredictable exposures (especially those emanating from the often-irrational United States tort system) and the complex insurance regulatory environment.

Ensuring Long-Term Profitability and Financial Strength

One of the greatest threats to an insurance company's balance sheet is a catastrophic event, manmade or natural, that destroys multiple structures or injures hundreds of people. Prudent insurers manage this threat by aggressively monitoring and managing their aggregate exposure to threats such as floods, hurricanes, earthquakes and terrorist attacks.

Such monitoring is designed to ensure that the carrier does not assume too large an exposure to any potentially large-scale loss in any particular part of the United States or the world. For example, an insurer may monitor carefully how many homes or buildings it insures in high-risk coastal areas or its workers' compensation exposure in congested cities vulnerable to high-fatality terrorist attacks. It models the "probable maximum loss" it could incur in these areas to ensure that the magnitude of potential losses does not exceed a certain percentage of its capital base.

A second major challenge to an insurer's long-term profitability—and viability—is systematic under-pricing. Some companies price (or under-price) to gain market share or do not have the expertise required to price risks appropriately. As a result, they may not collect sufficient premiums from customers to respond to eventual losses. In these circumstances, the company's underwriting risk will exceed its financial capacity. The company's financial strength will be severely shaken, and, eventually, insolvency may even result.

Insurers are especially vulnerable to the pitfalls of under-pricing not only because of competitive pricing pressures, but because the insurance industry, uniquely, does not know its "cost of goods," or the future losses to be paid out and must, therefore, project its cost of goods. Other industries, such as manufacturing, price products based on intimate knowledge of the component costs of production at the time the product is sold.

A third risk to insurer profitability emanates from an insurer's practice of investing funds that will eventually be needed to pay future losses. A company may invest substantial amounts in equities or bonds and rely too heavily on investment income, rather that underwriting profit, to make money. If the chosen investments do not perform well, the company could suffer significant losses.

Regulators monitor insurer's investment risk, keeping companies from being overly aggressive in investment practices and minimizing the risk of investment losses and the repercussions such losses could have for policyholders (i.e., the carrier's inability to pay claims). As a result, most insurance companies invest significant amounts in investment-grade fixed income securities, treasury bills and corporate and municipal bonds. Most insurers invest much smaller amounts in the generally riskier equities market.

Managing Unpredictable Exposures

Claims will erupt in the future from policies written in the present. Predicting this future exposure is difficult. The most glaring difficulty is posed by the United States tort system, which is prone to doling out unpredictable and often widely excessive damage awards, much of which end up being shouldered by insurers. Yet a liability insurer must predict today what the payout will be on a certain liability claim that may not occur for five or ten years down the road.

Further complicating this task, the payment for a particular injury or liability varies greatly across the United States based on the jurisdiction, the judge and the jury at hand. Liability for an injury litigated today in Texas may cost a corporation and its insurer five times more than the same injury litigated in Minnesota.

Moreover, exposures are constantly changing and new exposures emerging. Who would have thought, just a few years ago, that mold would become the looming liability issue it is today? After analyzing claim frequency and severity trends, judicial and regulatory dynamics and shifting economic and political environments, underwriters must do the best they can at assessing a fair price today to cover losses that may be incurred tomorrow. At no time is the experience and expertise of an underwriter more critical.

Navigating Myriad Regulations

Insurance is regulated state-by-state. Fifty regulators with fifty different sets of rules create significant bureaucracy for the insurance industry and a challenge for national insurers that must keep up to date on the legal and regulatory issues governing each state in which they operate. This complexity is compounded when an insurer operates globally and must also navigate the varied regulatory and legal issues in countries worldwide. An insurer must maintain a current, in-depth understanding of the regulatory and legal environments in which it operates. This adds to the complexity of the insurance business and, ultimately, insurance rates reflect this complexity.

Changes in the Insurance Industry

The insurance industry has changed over the past decade. Risks and insurance solutions have become larger, more numerous and more complex. Consequently, insurers and insurance buyers have adopted more sophisticated approaches to managing risk. "Risk sharing," for example, has become increasingly common, with businesses and individuals retaining more risk through high deductibles to manage the cost of insurance.

More and better tools and data are now available to support insurers in assessing and pricing risks. Current techniques for modeling exposures, such as hurricanes and earthquakes, are leaps and bounds ahead of where they were a decade ago.

Technology and the Internet have made deeper statistical data readily available to underwriters, enhancing underwriting and service to customers. Claims and engineering services have also progressed with the advancement of technology, enabling information to be shared in real time and claims to be reported 24/7 from virtually anywhere.

What Does the Future Hold?

Insurance provides financial certainty. Without insurance, commerce would cease and individuals would face undue financial hardship. Insurance is an industry that is essential and will remain essential.

It is also an evolutionary industry. As risks continue to grow and change and the specter of catastrophic losses remains, the industry will continue to adjust to these changing needs. It will innovate to help businesses and individuals better manage an increasingly uncertain world.

Consequently, new solutions will continue to emerge. Technology will further elevate the service insurers offer customers and the precision with which insurers can assess and rate risks.

Yet, one thing in this business will not change, and that is the importance of focusing on the fundamentals. Insurers must continue to zero-in on areas in which they have the expertise to succeed long term. To do this, they must nurture the professional talent and expertise that is the real engine driving this industry. Those who do this well will reap the greatest rewards from this business of risk.

Mr. Iordanou is president and chief executive officer of Arch Capital Group Ltd. (ACGL). He was previously chief executive officer of Arch Capital Group (U.S.) Inc., a wholly owned subsidiary of ACGL. Before joining Arch in December 2001, Mr. Iordanou was chief executive officer of Zurich U.S. and chief operating officer and chief executive officer of Zurich North America. He also served in various other capacities at Zurich Financial Services and its affiliates, including president of Zurich-American Specialties Division and senior executive vice president of group operations and business development of Zurich Financial Services. He was president of the commercial casualty division of the Berkshire Hathaway Group and senior vice president of American Home Assurance Company, a member of the American International Group.

A Glimpse Behind the Scenes

James J. Maguire
Chairman & Founder
Philadelphia Consolidated Holding Corp.

Insurance Business Basics

The insurance business is a profession, lke medicine, law, architecture and engineering. It is a business based on statistical probabilities and client-specific operating history.

Insurance transfers the risk of loss due to fortuitous or accidental events by pooling the resources of many for the unfortunate few. The insurance company benefits by charging adequate premium rates to cover its payments for these losses and the expenses of its operations. Insureds benefit by transferring their risk of loss.

Many insureds have, at most, a casual understanding of the actuarial probabilities that establish premium rates and have limited knowledge of the staggering amount of fraud that is inherent in the insurance business. Premium rates are established by the class (type) of risk. These rates are actuarially determined, based on the probability of expected claim frequency and severity of losses for exposures within a given class of risk. An example is professional liability coverage for the legal profession— lawyers. There are different premium rates for plaintiff attorneys who practice courtroom litigation versus estate planning attorneys who do not practice courtroom litigation. Another example of a class would be real estate attorneys.

An insured's risk is determined, in part, based on their history of losses, usually over the past three full years. If a law firm in the business of providing estate planning has had twelve claims in the prior three years, this is obviously not a risk a "sound" underwriter would initially consider at any premium rate. However, if all twelve claims came from the practice of one attorney who was no longer with the firm, an underwriter may entertain offering a premium rate.

When a claim is made for a loss payment, a claims adjustor will meet with the claimant to evaluate the loss and make a report to the insurance company. The company determines if the claim is covered under the terms of the insurance contract and, if it is, will remit payment for the loss. If it is determined that, under the terms of the insurance policy, the loss is partially covered, the company will negotiate a settlement.

The major players in the insurance industry include primary insurers licensed by the states where they conduct business, re-insurers, surplus lines insurers, rating agencies and regulators. Each player performs an independent but interconnecting role in the industry.

The Role of Re-Insurers

Primary insurers issue insurance policies directly to individuals and businesses. Re-insurers provide insurance coverage to primary insurers by charging a premium rate and providing insurance for specified losses of the primary company.

Industry standards define the amount of premium a prudent insurance company can underwrite given its policyholders' surplus. To underwrite more than three times, the company's surplus has historically proven to be risky for the continued financial health of a company.

Each year insurance companies are required to file their statutory financial statements in the states in which they are licensed. One immediate red flag for state regulators reviewing these financial reports is the ratio of written premium to surplus or capital. Insurance regulators are interested in the financial health of insurance companies licensed in their respective states for the obvious reason of ensuring that the company will have the ability to pay claims for the citizens of the state in the event of a loss under their insurance policy. To manage its premium writings in excess of this premium to surplus standard, a primary company can contract with a reinsurance company to transfer a certain level of premium writings (along with the risk), which would keep the ratio within the prescribed or desired standard. For example, an insurance company issues a $5 million liability policy and desires to hold only $1 million of the risk. The company would transfer $4 million of premium and associated risk to a re-insurer.

Such re-insurers cannot issue an insurance policy directly to a consumer or commercial entity, since only licensed insurers are permitted to issue insurance policies within the states they are licensed.

Re-insurers also provide capacity to primary companies. For example, a primary insurer insures an all-risk property contract for $100 million of coverage. Given the capital of the primary insurer, the company may be prepared to retain the first $5 million of the risk and would "shop" the reinsurance market for one, two or even three re-insurers that would accept, for a premium, $95 million in excess of the first $5 million or a quota share of such risk, perhaps 90 percent or 95 percent of each loss on the entire contract. In this scenario, if the primary company issues a $100 million policy and lays off $95 million to a re-insurer, and the re-insurer becomes bankrupt and is unable to fulfill its loss payment obligations, the primary company will be responsible for the loss claim under the policy. I believe, therefore, that one of the biggest risks in the industry today is the credit risk of the re-insurers.

Surplus Lines Companies

Exposures may be presented to insurance companies on which they are unwilling to offer premium and risk coverage terms. An example:

Guaranteeing the health of Citation, the racehorse. A surplus lines company will typically draft an insurance contract on unusual exposures, like the above, and have the unbridled luxury to offer an insurance policy and a premium rate not subject to insurance department regulation, as licensed primary insurers' policy forms and premium rates are.

The surplus line companies are not licensed by states, are known as non-admitted and provide insurance coverage that is not available from a licensed company. The type of insurance surplus lines companies write cannot be purchased through licensed companies.

Another example would be insuring against having a heart attack. One may be able to buy this type of insurance through a surplus lines company. The surplus line company, in determining the premium rate to charge and coverage to provide, takes a blank piece of paper, in essence, and writes up a contract. It can charge $10,000 or $100,000; the rate is up to the insurer since the state does not control it.

On the other hand, states control what licensed carriers can charge, and hence, licensed insurers can't arbitrarily charge $5,000 for your auto insurance. The premium rate charged to you is based on such criteria as where you live, your age and the number of prior accidents you have had. All the criteria utilized in determining the premium is regulated by the state. Surplus lines companies have no such regulation.

Rating Agencies

A.M. Best is the major rating agency for the insurance industry, though there are others. Rating agencies examine the financial strength of a company, and based on their examination, issue an appropriate rating, from A+ + (superior) all the way down to F (in liquidation), distinguishing the relative financial strength of companies.

The rating agencies have developed various financial ratios to determine the relative financial strength of a company. In an extreme example, for illustrative purposes, if a company recorded $5 billion in insurance premiums and had $1 billion in surplus, the company would have a premium to surplus ratio of 5 to 1 or $5 billion of premium against $1 billion of surplus.

With these numbers in mind, the rating agency would immediately examine the company very carefully due to its extreme premium to surplus leverage ratio. Based upon historical data, rating agencies require premium to surplus leverage ratios, at the extreme, to be below 3 to 1. An A+ company's requirement would be less than 2 to 1. The rating agencies constantly run different types of financial models, and, hence, companies must submit financial data to the rating agencies every quarter.

As another example, let's assume that in 1999, $500 million in reserves are recorded for future claim payments. Claims are not paid on the first day they are submitted to an insurance company, and, as a result, the company records a liability or a reserve for the expected ultimate amount that will be paid in the future for each claim.

The $500 million in reserves represents the company's estimate of what it will take to settle all the claims that occurred in, say, the year 1999. As the claims are paid out over time, A. M. Best ratios are calculated on how the claims are being paid by the Company. If it turns out that the claims actually paid for 1999 were $700 million—not $500 million—it is an indication to the rating agency that the company was not establishing sufficient reserves upon its initial evaluation of a claim. Potentially such factors could take a rating from an A+ down to an A or a B.

State Regulators

Rating agencies are always monitoring insurance companies. In addition to their constant vigilance, the regulators—the insurance departments of each state—monitor the rating agencies for their opinions about companies in their state. For instance, if the rating agency determines the financial ratios and warrants a B rating for a company, the insurance regulators would immediately review the company to determine the financial viability of the company in the interest of protecting the policyholders within their state.

A recent example of the above was the Reliance Insurance Co., which was licensed in all fifty states. When the company entered liquidation, it left $7 billion in claims for which it did not have the ability to pay. Needless to say, the insurance departments in all the states were very upset because of the resultant damage to their citizens.

Greatest Risks

Insurance is a business of risk, and risk can be miscalculated in many fashions. Examples of miscalculations that can be costly are reinsurance instability, flawed actuarial assumptions, inadequate premium rates, lax underwriting criteria, overly aggressive marketing, poor accounts receivable collection practices from insureds and re-insurers and flawed internal operating practices. Examples of these miscalculated risks follow:

Reinsurance Instability or Failure

Assume a primary insurer issues terms on a $50 million liability insurance policy to the Philadelphia Airport and reinsures $40 million of this coverage. Should the airport subsequently submit a claim of $50 million, the primary insurer will be liable for the claim payment of the $50 million to the airport and then must collect $40 million from its re-insurer under its reinsurance agreement. Obviously, if the re-insurer can't or won't pay, the primary company not only suffers the entire loss, but also loses the premium paid to the re-insurer.

Insurance companies must determine the financial strength of its re-insurers to alleviate the occurrence of this situation. Many times liability losses are paid four or five years or more after the insurance contract has expired. Companies have to know that their re-insurer will be able to pay under the terms of the reinsurance contract.

Flawed Actuarial Assumptions and Inadequate Rates

The determination of premium rates for a given class of business is based upon assumptions. As an example, let's examine the premium rate for the Domino's Pizza account. In this account, thousands of autos are used to deliver pizzas, and usually they are private passenger cars. Determining the premium rate as a private-passenger business-class car could be costly for this exposure, given the possibility of youthful drivers driving at night, in the city, rushing to get the pizza delivered hot.

Lax Underwriting Criteria and Overly Aggressive Marketing

The underwriting of commercial insurance is an art form that depends heavily on science and discipline. To adequately evaluate a risk, one must have complete information about the account—that is, loss history for three full years, financial history, type and amount of business and number of employees—and the discipline to obtain complete information.

Aggressive marketing can side step the underwriting procedures and seek shortcuts for the sake of making a sale. A disciplined operating procedure guards against shortcuts for the sake of marketing success.

Lax Accounts Receivable Management

With regard to collection from re-insurers, companies can and do have hundreds or even thousands of reinsurance contracts in force. Effective procedures must be in place to collect per the terms of these contracts.

In 1987, Integrity Insurance Company was declared insolvent by the New Jersey Insurance Department because it had allowed uncollected reinsurance to grow to a staggering $500 million. Integrity had allowed its records and procedures to deteriorate to such a state that it couldn't support or collect its receivables.

Companies hedge the above noted risks through financial controls, careful selection of reinsurance, outside audits, control of aggressive marketing, strict internal operating procedures, price monitoring, and non-negotiable underwriting codes.

Insurance Companies' Biggest Money Makers

Insurance companies make the greatest profit when they sell insurance and pay no claims.

There are ten categories of risk in every class of business. The categories run from 10 (the most risky) to 1 (the least risky). In the insurance industry, companies writing for low-risk categories are the real profit makers.

As an example, in the medical profession, the riskiest insurance policy is brain surgery. A midwife may be classified as a 4 because the risk is not quite so high. The receptionist in a doctor's office may be a 1.

For any industry or class of business, insurance companies can consult manuals that contain actuarial studies specifying the risk level of a certain class of business. Some insurance companies may decide to write risk class 10 policies, but others decide they can get enough premium to make a profit by writing far less risky classes of business.

In underwriting at Philadelphia Insurance Companies, our philosophy is to select those classes that are rated 1 to 6. We generally don't write business if the risk classification is above 6. We have a very conservative approach to the underwriting business. We analyze risk by classification. For example, we write insurance on certain social service organizations. Certain of these organizations are a 2 in risk classification. These organizations have property to insure and liability needs such as covering risk of slips and falls on their property and workers' compensation needs. But all of these risks are very low. The premium for this class of business is historically $4,000 to $5,000. The premium is not large, but there are not many claims, either.

Our company *could* write a hospital for an $800,000 premium—a large premium—but we think the risk is too great. When we analyzed it, we decided we would rather have 1,000 risks at $4,000 each than one big risk at $800,000 or $900,000. Three years from now, the hospital could have $3 million in claims, and we'd have only $900,000 in premiums, so we would have taken quite a loss.

In addition to simply selling new policies, insurance companies make money through good service, which creates repeat buyers. Insurance companies also carefully invest the premium received from policies to earn a reasonable return and have investments mature to match the timeframe in which it will be paying claims.

Determining the Premium

Premium rates for a new customer are determined by first looking at the class of business. For instance, the premium rate that is filed with a state reflects that x number of dollars will be charged for liability insurance for law firms. For example, $200 will be charged for each lawyer in a law firm, and, if there are ten lawyers in a law firm, 10 x $200, or $2,000 will be charged.

From the filed rate, a variance may be charged such as 25 percent more or 25 percent less, given extenuating circumstances. Extenuating circumstances could be that the ten lawyers have been in business for five years and have never had a claim, in which case as much as 25 percent credit may be applied to the filed premium rate with the state. Insurers make notes in underwriting files, such as the fact that an insured never had a claim in five years and that the filed rate with the state is $2,000 and that the filing with the state indicates up to 25 percent credit may be applied against this rate. Conversely, if the insured had two or three claims in the past three years, the insurer may surcharge the account 25 percent, annotating the file accordingly.

All deviations from filed rates are maintained in files, since each state has the right to examine files to confirm insurance carriers are charging premium rates in accordance with their filed rates. If the state auditors arrive to audit the files and find an insurer has given credits or surcharges without valid reasons for doing so, the insurer may have to pay a fine; hence, one has to be careful that debits and credits are done in accordance with reasonable underwriting standards.

Reserves and Investments

At Philadelphia Insurance, we will do about $1.1 billion in business. When premiums are received, the funds are immediately invested. We invest 90 percent of the premium amounts received in the bond market and 10 percent in the equity market. This is fairly conservative, but we want to ensure that money will be available when it is time to pay the claims. Hence, the money is invested in relatively short instruments that earn us a return; we don't invest in thirty-year bonds.

When we are notified of a claim, a reserve representing the estimate of the future ultimate loss payment is established. It usually takes anywhere from twenty-four to sixty months to pay a claim. Some property damage claims or collision damage claims are easy and are paid in six months. But larger and more complex claims take time to investigate to determine the extent of the claim payment.

Processing a Claim

A commercial liability claim will be used as an example to explain the claim process. Let's say a policyholder has a beauty salon where a customer has tripped and fallen, suffering an injury. The afflicted individual claims that the salon owner was negligent because a rug at the front door caused the fall.

The first action undertaken by the insurance company upon being notified of the claim is to have a claim adjuster visit the salon to determine if, in fact, the salon was negligent in any fashion.

The next step is to speak to the injured party, and if a doctor was involved, to speak to the doctor and obtain the medical records.

A claim settlement then would be negotiated with the injured party taking into account the medical costs incurred; the amount of time missed from work and the extent of pain, suffering and anguish incurred. Claims are settled through negotiations with the claimant, which is typical of the way in which most claims are handled.

Another example would be a case where a roof blows off a building. In this case, a contractor would be sent to inspect the roof and file a report with the insurance company. Perhaps it is estimated that it will cost $600,000 to put a new roof on this building as a result of the structure being damaged. Contractors would be requested to submit bids for completing the repairs. These bids would be reviewed by claims staff members at Philadelphia Insurance Company, who have contractor experience and the technical expertise to settle this type of claim.

Succeeding in the Insurance Business

Marketing insurance products is critical for success. An insurance company has much to offer other than price; in fact, selling on price is a sure remedy for failure. Insurers differentiate themselves in a variety of ways, including product, service, financial stability, history of operations and expertise in certain lines of business.

Philadelphia Insurance Company's strategy is straightforward in that we provide local representation and a contract that offers more and better coverage than our competition at rates that are fair but not the lowest. This is coupled with a financial strength rating of A+, which says we will be here to pay if there is a claim. I tell my employees to show up each day, follow our business plan and stick to our code of conduct. The rest will take care of itself.

The best insurance business advice I ever received was not to focus on top-line growth but to concentrate on sound and solid underwriting results. Success in the insurance industry is a direct result of having the discipline to walk away from unprofitable business and to stick to underwriting criteria and adequate pricing even when competitors are willing to cut their rates.

I measure the success of our business and of the employees in our business by the professionalism they demonstrate in doing their jobs daily. Financial measurements and the fact that we are a billion-dollar company are, of course, good measurements, but I think professionalism is a key element for realizing success.

We see professionals, like doctors, lawyers, architects and engineers, as role models. I believe an insurance company is successful when it goes about its work as professionally as it possibly can, and I preach the same to the employees of my company. The bottom line profit will come. Concentrate on professionalism every day, and, one day, you will find more profit than you expected to have, in a business with great financial strength.

If you want to be successful in the insurance business, I believe you must follow three rules:

1. Don't compromise actuarial pricing;
2. Know your insured and the exposure you're insuring;
3. Know the financial strength of your re-insurers.

I have seen too many companies get starry-eyed about premium, but premium is only one part of the puzzle. After you collect the premium dollars, you must pay the claims and expenses. What is left over is what makes a company successful. Too many companies are shortsighted, believing they will invest the big premium dollars wisely, and with the investment income and the underwriting, they will make huge profits.

I don't think that is the way to go about seeking success. Top-line growth, premium growth, is not the answer. When you write business, you have to constantly focus on the probabilities of losses and profits from every piece of business.

In our business, you can be bankrupt and not know it for three or four years, until all the claims have been reported. After you collected and invested all the premiums, suddenly, you realize you haven't made enough incremental investment income to pay for the claims as a result of poor underwriting. That's certainly true today with investment interest rates at 3.5 percent. My advice is to guard against going after premium in favor of going after profitable business.

Insurance Industry Challenges

I believe that the biggest challenge in the insurance industry today is to maintain the discipline of your business plan.

We have a business plan that states we will not take a risk greater than category 6. We have to guard against getting starry-eyed about an $800,000 or $900,000 premium account with a greater risk category than 6. We must maintain the discipline!

Another big risk, in my opinion, is purchasing reinsurance. It is critical that the reinsurance company is financially sound and will be there when you call on them to pay a claim.

The reinsurance bill at our company is about $75 million per year. We buy reinsurance on all liability in excess of $1 million; on all umbrella policies, we underwrite up to $10 million. On the property insurance we underwrite, we retain $2 million of exposure and buy reinsurance for any exposure in excess of this amount.

I could purchase reinsurance for less, saving, as an example, $25 million a year, but I would have to purchase it from carriers that are not rated highly by A.M. Best, and I won't do that.

Changes in the Insurance Business

In recent years, the major change in the industry has been depletion of industry capital and the failure of what were considered stable companies. Industry capital has suffered depletion due to staggering losses resulting from 9/11, asbestos litigation, tobacco litigation and medical malpractice litigation, which today has driven a number of insurance companies out of that business.

Workers' compensation losses have risen far beyond predictions, in large part because of malingering and fraudulent claims that purport that workers are unable to return to their jobs or any other job. In these cases, work ers' compensation insurance continues to pay.

There is a mentality in America today, spawned, in large, part by unscrupulous lawyers, that an accident or an injury creates the opportunity to hit the jackpot against the insurance company. Falling on that rug in the beauty salon and bruising an elbow could be litigated into a staggering award by a jury.

In addition to these pitfalls, insurance companies have suffered severe investment losses in recent years, not only in the stock market: The yield on fixed-income securities is at its lowest point in forty years. Insurance companies can no longer earn enough return on their premiums to offset the above noted issues.

In the 45 years I've been in business, I've seen between 50 and 100 bankruptcies. Household names are going out of business. Reliance Insurance Company, a 100-year-old institution, declared bankruptcy and is now being liquidated by the Pennsylvania Insurance Department. Kemper Insurance Company, Legion Insurance Company and Frontier Insurance Company, once all multi-billion-dollar companies, are out of business, and their insureds are left with contracts of insurance that can't pay on losses.

The reinsurance industry has seen its fair share of companies go out of business as well. For example, Mutual Risk, Trenwick, Gerling and PMA Re. Lloyds of London, supposedly an institution of great strength, recently called on its member owners to infuse billions of fresh capital into the company to stay afloat.

Because of the difficulties companies face today, there has been a movement afoot for the stronger companies to acquire the weaker. As for insolvencies, state insurance departments are moving much more quickly today to take control of financially borderline companies. Additionally, they have stepped up their examination practices. Instead of sending regulators sporadically, today, they are immediately present with the slightest indication of an unbalanced risk profile.

It's interesting to note that fewer than five percent of the pooled companies in the insurance industry today are rated A+ by A.M. Best, down from 24 percent five years ago.

The Next Five to Ten Years

Over the next five to ten years, we will see consolidation continue as companies merge with each other to gain financial strength. Also, we will see more problems in the industry because companies are not adequately reserved for the claims they have on their books. That will cause the downgrading of companies from a rating standpoint. We will see companies suffer from the loss of capital by virtue of additional claims.

At the same time, for the financially "clean" companies, there will be some interesting opportunities. With companies failing and being downgraded, the financially strong companies will have it more their way in the business they are writing. Philadelphia Insurance is an A+ carrier and can select the business that meets our underwriting criteria, charge adequate rates for this business and turn away the business that doesn't meet our risk profile. That is how the financially strong companies will survive in the future, with the financially weak companies falling by the wayside or merging with the stronger companies.

Mr. Maguire founded Maguire Insurance Agency, Inc. in 1960 and incorporated in 1962. In 1980, Mr. Maguire formed a holding company, which today is publicly traded under the name "Philadelphia Consolidated Holding Corp." (NASDAQ – PHLY).

The holding company owns (one hundred percent) four subsidiaries: Maguire Insurance Agency, Inc. is an insurance marketing Agency licensed in all States. Philadelphia Insurance Company is domiciled in Pennsylvania and approved to write surplus lines insurance in thirty-seven states. Philadelphia Indemnity Insurance Company is domiciled in Pennsylvania and licensed to write property and casualty insurance in all states. Liberty American Insurance Group is the holding company for two personal lines insurance companies domiciled in Florida, Liberty American Insurance Company and Mobile USA Insurance Company.

The insurance companies, as a group and individually, are rated "A + (Superior)" by A.M. Best Company, a rating held by only five percent of the 3,350 U.S. insurance companies. The company is also rated by Standard & Poor's as "A" in claims paying ability and underwrites specialty commercial and personal property and casualty insurance products through its thirty-six proprietary underwriting offices located across the United States.

Mr. Maguire received a MaB.S. Degree from Saint Joseph's University 1958, after serving in the United States Army in Korea from June 1954 to June 1958.

Mr. Maguire and Frances M. Maguire live in Chestnut Hill, Philadelphia at the same address as they have for the past thirty-four years and are the parents of eight children (three boys and five girls) ranging in age from twenty-nine to forty-two.

A People Business

Robert V. James
President & COO
Balboa Insurance Group

The Basics of the Insurance Industry

Insurance is one of the few products sold today where the actual justification for pricing happens two to fifteen years *after* the policy is purchased.

It has always been the main issue for insurance companies. We set prices for a product that really will not be paid out for several years. The clie nt buys the product today, but the claims happen in the future, and even though you have historical experience to measure claims results, they're not always accurate. Pragmatically, from the insurance company's perspective, what the firm tries to do is to assess the risk that it's taking with any given client and charge a price that's got a little bit of margin in it for a profit.

The predictive and not always accurate business model is integral and is also one of the things that makes the insurance industry endemically unprofitable for a lot of companies. It's why the insurance industry has had such poor margins over the years; it's difficult to predict what the actual results are on a book of business that you write.

Assessing Risk

The insurance industry uses a host of statistical measures that are all bound up in the phrase "actuarial profession." Companies look at past losses for similar risks and then try to take those past trends and predict them into the future, adding on things like cost of inflation and investment income to try to determine—based upon the past—how much money they have to charge for a product in the future.

Pricing a premium is one basic process for an insurance company. Generally speaking, a company will look either at their own historical data for that class of business, or use some industry data that is aggregated by independent service organizations. The company will come up with an assessment; say $700 for a particular class of business. Then, it will take that $700 and add to it what expense costs will be, along with some margin for profit. The company may determine that, for the class of business, it must charge $1,075, and, then, as it writes business in those classes, it will modify that assessment structure based upon actual experience.

The most difficult aspect of the business is risk mitigation and properly pricing for the product, because there are so many moving parts, both in terms of loss trends and investment trends, that the industry generally doesn't get it right. If you go back and look at historical data from the industry, it goes through these pricing cycles where for many, many years it will tend to lose money. Then, it will get to a point where it loses so much money that it will decide it can't do that any more, so everybody starts raising prices, and they get healthy for about three or four years, and then they go back. It's cyclical in nature. That's probably the thing that the industry finds hardest to do, mitigate risk to smooth out cyclicality and stick to a pricing and underwriting discipline that will lead to long-term profitability.

The Process of Processing

Processing claims is another important aspect of the business. Most claims are filed by the customer who has the policy, although some claims are filed by the person the customer allegedly injured. The claim process generally works like this: we will get a first notice of loss, which is some basic information about the nature of the loss, who was involved in it, what happened and some basic circumstances around the loss. There will then be a brief investigation to verify that we do, in fact, insure that customer and that that the policy covers that type of loss. Then a claim file will be set up, saying that we will have to pay this claim to one extent or another, and an initial reserve will be set up on that file, which simply means the claims adjustor will look at the circumstances of the loss and say, "I think this loss is going to cost the company $10,000, so I'll set up a reserve for that amount." There are some companies that set up "formula based" case reserves. That simply means that they have designed a set of business rules that sets up the reserves with a predetermined amount for that type of loss at the initial claim file setup. In either case, the reserves are adjusted as time goes on and more is known about the nature and extent of the loss.

From that point in time, the company goes through the rest of the investigation to determine what the actual damages are and what we have to do to put the customer in the same position that they were in before the loss. Then we start paying the money to do so.

On a property loss, where you're just replacing property—you've got a claim for a stolen TV—these are fairly easy to resolve, to burned-down homes, which are more complicated. They're both under the same principal, though. You're just trying to restore the customer to where he or she was, and it's fairly easy to define, because you're dealing with a tangible loss of property.

On a liability loss, where there are allegations that the insured injured somebody else, then how much that injury is worth and whether there is litigation involved makes it more complicated, but the philosophy is basically the same. Relatively speaking, property losses get settled more quickly than liability losses. Another maxim, generally speaking, is the larger the loss, the longer it takes to settle, because, generally, size equates to complexity of the loss.

Ensuring Profitability

I think the broad perception among the average consumer is that customers pay a lot for their insurance, and they don't get anything back unless they have a claim. And when they have a claim, they get hassled by the insurance company.

I also think the common belief is that insurance companies just make tons of money at the expense of the consumer. But when you look at the results of the insurance industry over the last twenty to forty years, what you find is that the product itself has little margin. If you take in a dollar of premium, depending on the company and the line of business, twenty-five to thirty cents of that dollar pays for the company's expenses, the rest of it goes out for losses, and there's little money left over in that dollar of premium that the insurance company would consider profit.

A lot of insurance companies will actually do what we call "underwrite to a loss." In other words, they'll take in a dollar of premium and expect to pay out more than a dollar in losses and expenses, but they'll hope to make it up in investment income.

So, in terms of how it works for the consumers, what's happening inside the insurance company is most of the money is being paid out in losses. The mitigating factor, in terms of trying to hold down prices on insurance, is to try to select risks that have a lower propensity for loss and, also, to try to invest this premium that you're collecting in as high an interest rate product as you can that is still safe to get the investment income. Once you get past those cost-mitigating factors, the rest of the insurance product is, frankly, driven by whatever's going on from a societal perspective. Nowadays, it is a runaway litigation environment where everybody sues everybody.

Some companies also make money by extending their insurance paper to other entities. Let's say that you own a large corporation, and you want to self-insure your workers' compensation coverage for your employees, because you're a large business. But in order to do that, you still have to issue a workers' comp insurance policy, because the state requires it, and you're not an insurance company.

You might go to an insurance company and say, "I'm going to self-insure my workers' comp. Here's how I'm going to do it from a financial perspective: I need to issue a policy on your paper, and I will pay you a fee (called a fronting fee) to use your paper, but I'm going to take care of the losses on the back end." A fronting fee is generally a small percentage, so if they're writing $100 in premium, the fronting fee might be 9 to 10 percent of that, or $9 to $10.

Profitability is the biggest thing I focus on as the company leader. That's pretty much everything, because you're dealing with a business that has thin margins, and it doesn't take much to turn those positive margins into negative margins.

There are a few major factors in determining success in this business, and profitability would be number one. Top-line growth would be number two, how much you are growing your premium base. Number three would be market share growth, how big you are relative to your competition. Number four would be your customer satisfaction measures. Number five would be measures of what the Departments of Insurance say about you, because they come in and do market conduct exams where they actually audit your business.

The Many Faces of Risk

There are a lot of risks an insurance company faces. One category is investment risk. Companies collect all this money, and then they try to invest it in the marketplace to try to earn investment income. The mitigating factors around investment risk are that most insurance companies take an extremely conservative investment posture. We primarily invest in government bonds, in things that have traditionally been extremely low risk.

Another category of risk would be catastrophe risk, whether it's natural catastrophe or whether it's the newest form of catastrophe, which is terrorism. Insurance companies try to mitigate those risks in a number of ways. One is to get a spread of business so you don't have all your business concentrated in catastrophe-prone areas, and then, secondly, to purchase re-insurance from companies that basically sell insurance to insurance companies for that catastrophe risk, so you can remove some of the volatility. The problem that the insurance industry has with the terrorism issue is that terrorism re-insurance is not readily available, and, when it is, it's extremely expensive. There is no real historical data set to predict when or where it's going to happen.

The other type of risk that comes to mind for insurance companies to deal with is changes in mass torts, for example, the asbestos issue. Now you have people who are suing McDonald's because they say McDonald's made them fat. You've got the class action lawsuits, the mold in homes issues; you get these large mass tort legal issues going on that the policies never really contemplated as a risk that would have to be covered when the policies were written, so the policies were never priced that way.

Companies, generally speaking, can only mitigate that risk after the fact. If, for example, you know that mold is going to become an issue because you're paying out claims on it, then what you do is you exclude mold coverage from your policies. But that doesn't do much for all the exposure that you have underwritten over the course of those preceding years.

The last thing that comes to mind is regulatory risk. The insurance industry is regulated by the states, not the federal government. As states go through their normal political changes, they can become a more onerous environment in which to do business. The ways that the companies try to mitigate those risks are to understand what the regulatory environment is, influence it through lobbying and manage relationships with the states' departments of insurance. For those marketplaces that are extremely onerous from a regulatory standpoint, companies try to minimize the amount of business they do in those marketplaces, in the worst case scenario, to withdraw from those markets altogether.

Customer Relations and Marketing

How you go about getting new customers depends upon the kind of insurance company you are. There are some companies, like Geico, in particular, that are "direct marketing companies," so they are appealing directly to the consumer. They ask the consumer to interact with them either over the Internet, which is a fairly new phenomenon, or through a call-center.

Then there are companies that tend to do business through agents, who are really out soliciting business. In the agency environment, there are, generally speaking, two kinds of agents. There's the agent that represents one company, which would be something like State Farm or Allstate.

Then there are agents that represent multiple companies, known as independent agents.

If you're Allstate or State Farm, the idea is to hire and train the best agents you can and create incentives for them in a way to continue to want to grow their business, because you're the only company they can place business with. If you're doing business with independent agents, it's a similar thing in that you're trying to select the best independent agents, but then you have to provide them with a product that is compelling and support services that are much desired, so that they would rather choose your product than the other companies that they represent.

In the insurance business, those are the three primary ways that insurance companies that are selling to businesses would garner business for them selves.

Marketing is obviously important, but a lot of it is dependent on how you're getting business. For a company like Geico or Allstate, where they're trying to appeal directly to the customer, either through a captive agent or directly to the customer, market segmentation and customer buying habits are important. For a company that is doing business through independent agents—and the independent agent is really acting as the marketer for the company—I think marketing, in the traditional sense, is a little less important. Instead, it's more about the insurance company creating top-of-mind awareness for the agent versus for the customer, so your company's services are the ones the agent wants to sell.

Once we get those clients, we generally want to keep them. Maintaining a standard of excellence in terms of customer service is a priority. To do so, we use a lot of technology. We use call center technology to handle customer inquiries, electronic payment technology to streamline payment processing, Internet technology to extend our systems and information directly to agents and customers, and we use technology now to have some work done offshore to provide lower costs and 24/7 coverage. We try to build metrics, so we can measure customer service, and we use feedback mechanisms, like surveys, to try to gauge service.

Choosing an Insurance Provider

Selecting the right insurance company largely depends on the insurance product that someone's buying. Studies have found that companies that have asked market research questions like, "Why are you buying insurance from a particular company?" have generated comments like, "They were the lowest price," or "Price was a big motivator."

But I think it's more complex than that. I think that a lot of consumers today still rely on the advice of an insurance agent to make decisions. Even though they are concerned about what they perceive to be competitive pricing, I think the consumer that thinks about it is also concerned about, "Will the insurance company be around when they have a claim, and will they have the ability to pay my claim?" So, financial stability, service and company reputation in the marketplace for paying claims are all important. Those things all get wrapped up in an advertising campaign that is designed to tell consumers why those qualities are resident in the company.

Dealing With a Bad Rep

Unfortunately for the insurance industry, research suggests that the insurance industry is, from a reputation standpoint, down somewhere along with used car salespeople and lawyers. The industry suffers from a credibility problem in and of itself. We are selling an intangible product;

it's really no more than a stack of papers that has promises associated with it. It's written in legalese that the average consumer doesn't understand very well, and it's a product that nobody wants to purchase, that many people don't completely understand. On top of that, they don't really want to use the product because the only time they do is when something bad has happened to them. It's a combination of a lot of bad things.

I think what a company does to overcome that and gain credibility is to have good customer service, be fair and prompt in its claim practices, competitive in its pricing and to follow the "golden rule" as it interacts in the marketplace. Agents can explain what's in the policy and how it applies to clients. Probably most importantly, when the customer does, in fact, have a claim, they should handle it fairly and expeditiously, because that's really the moment of truth from the customer's perspective.

Bureaucratic and Legal Issues

The regulatory environment is probably the biggest source of bureaucratic problems for the industry. A large insurance company like Allstate is a national company, but it's regulated fifty different ways, because it's dealing with agencies at the state level, so it cannot have one approach to the marketplace for a particular kind of business. That's a bureaucracy that is, some would say, cumbersome.

Another bureaucracy, which I don't think is necessarily a bad bureaucracy, but it exists for all publicly owned companies, is the rating agencies that watch the financial stability and financial strength of companies and put guidelines around how much capital you can put out to grow your business. So, an insurance company has got to be cognizant of what those regulatory agencies are looking for in terms of capital strength before they decide to grow too quickly or get into lines of business that might be considered more volatile.

Keeping Current in the Industry

The industry doesn't do a really good job with keeping track of changes and making sure people are up-to-date. The agents certainly play a part in it, because they have the most face-to-face contact with customers. Insurance companies use a variety of communication tools to talk to customers, including inserts into their policy statements, inserts into their billing statements, newsletters, and so on The most recent phenomenon is the use of an Internet site to educate customers and e-mail marketing campaigns. Depending upon the nature of the business—for example, if you're Geico and you don't have an agency force—you may spend more time talking directly to a customer than if you're a company dealing through independent agents.

Of course, innovation is important, but the problem is you can only be innovative within the constraints of the regulatory and legal environments. At least traditionally, it's been difficult to have innovation last long, because the product is fairly easy to replicate. If I issue a policy, and I have to file it with the Department of Insurance, a competitor can go down to the Department of Insurance, read that policy and basically replicate the whole thing. So, it's difficult to hold innovation in the marketplace that the customer can really see as a differentiator for a long period of time.

Industry Changes and the Future of the Insurance Business

I think up until 9/11, nobody really considered those kinds of acts of terrorism as things that they had to plan for in the pricing of their product. It caused the industry to really try to think about how they were going to develop pricing models to deal with the terrorist threat.

Let me just draw a contrast: terrorism is a relatively new phenomenon, and it's a manmade phenomenon, so it's difficult to predict. We have many of ways to predict where hurricanes are going to strike, how severe the damage is going to be. We have fifty or seventy-five years of data on storm paths in the United States, so that you can say, "Gee, if you have a lot of business in Hilton Head, S.C., sooner or later, you're going to get hit with a hurricane."

Terrorism has a different set of parameters, and it's difficult to predict. So, you have all these companies that have all of this exposure that may be subject to acts of terrorism, and they have few ways to predict it. As a result, they have a limited ability to price for that exposure.

I think terrorism will continue to be problematic for the industry. I think technology will continue to make the industry more efficient, but I do believe that any gains that the insurance industry gets, in terms of their expenses ratio from improvements in technology, will be replaced with a continuing theme of "Let's litigate as a way to solve this problem." Litigation costs will continue to increase, and that will make insurance more expensive, not less expensive.

Courtroom activity also continues to shift the insurance landscape through what I call an "activist judiciary." Our policy may say, "We don't cover this type of loss," and the judge might say, "Well, we think that's against public policy; so, even though the policy doesn't cover it, we're going to make you pay it anyway," which makes it difficult for insurance companies to price their product.

One of the biggest problems that the United States economy has is this continuing rise in litigation costs. You can see it in the medical malpractice field, where you have doctors walking off the job because they can no longer afford to buy their malpractice insurance. Some of these awards, at least on the surface, appear to be ways for lawyers to make money. I think the issue of personal responsibility and taking responsibility for your own actions, rather than trying to blame them on somebody else, has become a societal problem for the United States that will make the country less and less competitive, vis-à-vis some of the other developing countries in the world that don't have the same kind of mentality that we do.

It has a direct impact on the insurance industry, because we have to end up paying those claims, but it has an impact on the American economy in general. If there was one thing I could change, it would be to get real live tort reform so you wouldn't have lawsuits that are either frivolous or force you to pay out much more than you really should pay from a damage standpoint.

The other external factor that has changed the industry is the change in the investment climate. As the investment dimate changes over the year, when investments go up or down, and you can look at the interest rates as a barometer for that, it changes the profitability index for the industry, because so much of their money gets invested in those kinds of instruments.

Advice

1) Do the right thing. In the face of pressure, to make an expedient choice, ask yourself two questions: Would your parents be proud of what you're about to do? Would you want this decision on the cover of the Wall Street Journal?

2) Protect the shareholder. After all, it is their money you are managing. At the end of the day, remember you can't manage a business for the long-term if you are always losing money in the short-term. Sooner or later, the long-term view has to be based upon consistently good short-term results.

3) Find really smart people, give them a vision and let them run. This business is about analyzing risk, and all of the computer models in the world won't replace really smart people.

4) Treat your people well. We live in a free enterprise system. Good people want to be treated well, compensated well, respected, and they want to contribute. If you don't treat them that way, they will leave and you will fail.

5) Be externally focused. Generally speaking, there is no one in your Home Office who is talking to the customer. Get out there and understand what it is like in their world. That includes your interactions with agents as well.

6) Practice being a good listener. This is hard, and something leaders don't always come to naturally.

7) Practice humility. Servant leadership is the best way to lead. Don't believe your own Public Relations; you're good, but, really, are you so good that you can't learn something from someone else?

8) Be nice to the mail-clerk, the janitor, the valet parking person. How you interact with those who can't help your career shows who you really are.

9) Slow down a little. Understand when real urgency is needed versus just being frantic. Most decisions need to be made with dispatch, but

mulling them for twenty-four hours won't kill the business and may lead to a more rational decision.

10) Stop the e-mail; pick up the phone; go see the person; write a handwritten note. Remember, this is, was and always will be a people business.

Mr. James is Managing Director for Countrywide Financial Corporation and serves as president and chief operations officer of Balboa Insurance Group (BIG).

Within BIG, James oversees business activities for the Balboa Life & Casualty Group, insurers who provide property and casualty and life insurance; Balboa Reinsurance Company, which provides reinsurance coverage to primary mortgage insurance companies that insure payment of mortgage loans; Countrywide Insurance Services, Inc., an independent insurance agency that provides consumers with homeowners and various other insurance products; and DirectNet, Inc., a full service third-party insurance agency.

Prior to joining Balboa, James served as executive vice president of U.S. Insurance Operations for CNA Insurance Companies, responsible for field operations and worldwide processing and billing operations. With twenty-five years of underwriting, operations, sales, marketing and technology experience, James also held management and sales positions with Allstate Insurance, MetLife Auto & Home, Allmerica Financial and American International Group.

The Road to Success in the Insurance Industry

William G. Star
Chairman, President, & Chief Executive Officer
Kingsway Financial Services Inc.

The Basics of the Insurance Business

The purpose of insurance is to spread the exposure of a person or corporation among many through a common entity. In the early days of the industry, it was a matter of ship owners arranging to each carry a portion of each other's cargo so that if one ship sank, a portion of the cargo owned by each ship owner would still be safe. In current times, risk is shared by a person paying a premium to an insurance company in return for the company agreeing to pay an agreed amount upon the occurrence of a certain event.

Premiums are usually determined on an actuarially sound basis to cover the risk accepted from the insured. In the case of automobile insurance, the average cost of claims is determined, along with the loss frequency and the cost of operations. The premium is developed to cover the overall cost of an insured group, and a small loading is applied for a profit margin. In the case of some lines of business in which the time between the payment of the premium and the expected time to pay a claim is substantial; then, an estimate of the investment income during that period of time can be used to reduce the premium level. In life insurance, the determination of the premium is based upon preexisting conditions, life expectancy and interest rates. In addition to that is a factor that is applied if there is an investment portion to provide a payment to the insured person at a specified period of time.

There are three major types of companies in the insurance industry. First, life insurance companies provide individual life insurance policies (both whole life, which includes savings, and term insurance, which provides a benefit only upon the death of the insured person), annuities, accident and sickness insurance, income protection, group coverage for employers and so on. Life companies include companies such as Mutual of New York (MONY), Allstate Life, Prudential, Manulife, Great West Life and Sun Life.

Second, property and casualty (P&C) insurance companies provide insurance for automobiles, trucks, taxis and motorcycles; liability insurance; surety; property insurance and personal property insurance, including jewelry, paintings, household goods and so on. P&C insurers include State Farm, Allstate, Geico, USAA, Progressive and Zurich.

Third, re-insurers accept risk from insurance companies and, thereby, spread the exposure among more companies. For example, if an insurance company issued a policy for $5 million but only wanted to keep an exposure of $1 million, the company would reinsure the other $4 million with a re-insurer. The re-insurer, in turn, may retrocede a portion of the $4 million to another re-insurer to reduce its exposure. Reinsurance companies include Munich, American Re, Swiss Re, General Re, and Zurich.

The Claim Process

To make a claim, in the case of life insurance, the beneficiary usually submits a death certificate to the insurer and completes the necessary claim forms. Property claims for burglary or fire are investigated to determine the actual value of the stolen or damaged property. It is then necessary to determine if fraud or arson is involved. Once the insurer is satisfied that the claim is legitimate, a "proof of loss" form is completed, signed and notarized. The claim is then paid within the prescribed time. In the case of liability insurance involving injured persons, from a car accident or a fall on premises, for example, the injuries are determined and then a settlement is offered after the damages are determined. If the offer is not satisfactory, then the settlement is usually decided by arbitration or by a court award.

In many cases there is a disagreement between the insured person and the insurer about the value of the stolen or damaged property. In the case of disagreement, both parties can agree to each have an appraiser determine the value involved and then have an arbitrator make a decision.

In the case of injuries, some will go to arbitration, but the majority of claims that are disputed are usually settled by the courts.

Risks

The three biggest risks insurance companies face are spread of risk, pricing and claims settlement. Spread of risk is important because a company must be concerned with having too much exposure at any given location. For example, with the World Trade Center, some companies were exposed to far more risk than they expected since they did not expect different business locations on different floors and in different buildings to be destroyed at one time. Even companies providing life, workers' compensation and health and accident insurance would not expect so many claims from such a location.

In the area of pricing, the problem is that insurance is sold at a specific price for a claim that may occur at a given time in the future. Since premiums are based on probability of loss, the cost of claims can change with future circumstances that could not be predicted at the time of the sale. Unlike a manufacturing business in which the cost of the materials and labor can be determined at the time of manufacture and priced accordingly, the cost of the insurance product is not determined until a future date. The most difficult aspect of the insurance business is pricing the product without being able to determine what new exposures might occur during the policy term.

Claims handling is also a great risk due to fraud and the uncertainty of the outcome of court decisions. In many cases, in automobile accidents where "no fault" coverage is available are staged accidents, and the occupants of the cars claim they are injured. In Canada, the province of Ontario has one of the worst records for fraud. Some paralegals and rehab clinics specialize in staged accidents and also work with tow truck drivers to divert people from the scene of the accident to their business locations. They tell people they will be able to collect benefits for their fictitious injuries. This practice is also common in Florida and New York State.

Court decisions are also unpredictable in dealing with soft tissue and psychological injuries, since an accurate diagnosis is not possible in most cases, and awards vary depending upon the preparation of the lawyers involved and the testimony of hired doctors. The appearance of the injured person will also influence the decision. In most cases of fraudulent claims and soft tissue injuries, the damage to the automobiles involved in the accident is minor.

Risks are hedged by the spread of risk, arrangement of reinsurance (to have other companies take a portion of the risk) and the actuarial determination of factors that can be taken into account in the pricing. A good hedge can also be diversification by product lines and geographic location.

Making a Profit

The greatest profits come from specialty lines of business in which there is limited competition. Surety business is usually a high-profit line, but losses in certain years have been extremely high. Motorcycle and nonstandard automobile insurance has been a high-profit line over the years and has rarely produced losses for specialty insurers. Product warranty business has also produced exceptional profit for companies that specialize in that class. Credit life and disability insurance has traditionally been an extremely good profit producer for insurers affiliated with banks or other financial institutions.

Insurers profit from the difference between the premiums they collect and the operating expenses and claims paid. Usually, the greatest amount of profit for an insurer is the investment income.

From the time insurance premiums are collected by an insurer until the time claims are paid, the money is invested in securities that pay interest or dividends. The majority of the money is kept in bonds or term deposits, but most companies will also invest in stocks. Companies will usually invest less than 25 percent of the funds in stocks, but it is not unusual for European insurers to go as high as 35 percent. That was the case prior to 2001, and when the stock market dropped in 2001, billions of dollars were lost. Companies are now taking a more conservative approach.

Most people would be surprised to find that most of the profit generated by insurers comes from investment income. Very little of the profit is from the risk exposure, and in many cases, especially with automobile insurers, the companies pay out more in expenses and claims than the premiums they collect. For every dollar of capital an insurer has, up to $2.75 of premiums can be written. In this way, an insurer has about three dollars to invest for every dollar of capital available. That is why the majority of income is derived from investment income. When interest rates are high, some insurers will reduce rates and have an underwriting loss in order to have a larger investment portfolio.

Another source of income is fees from re-insurers. Some companies will provide the policies but take no risk. The risk is transferred to a re-insurer and the re-insurer pays a fee for the issuance and servicing of the policy. Most re-insurers are not licensed to act as an insurer and cannot issue policies directly to the public. In cases where they want to become involved in certain lines of business, they will arrange to have an insurance company issue the policies, but the re-insurer will assume the entire risk. The insurance company will not have any risk. This is referred to as a fronting arrangement.

Differentiators

Companies will set premiums at different levels from each other depending upon their preference for a given type of risk. Reinsurance costs vary by company, and if a particular company finds the cost of reinsurance too great, it might refuse a class of risk or charge much higher premiums. Price is important to the consumer, but commercial buyers are interested in the rating of the company, as well as reputation for paying claims and flexibility in providing different types of policy coverage and terms.

Marketing is more important than pricing, even though most people are interested in the price. It is important to select markets that have usually been profitable and where the risk is better controlled. Development of reputation is important so that the salesperson, agent or broker can be confident, when he or she sells the policy, that the company will stay in business and pay future losses when a claim arises.

Insurance is tightly regulated by various forms of government. In most jurisdictions, rate and form approval is required. Insurance commissioners control the licensing of companies and set certain standards for capital requirements. They also conduct audits to determine if fair practices are maintained by insurance companies. Because automobile insurance is politically sensitive, governments often act unreasonably toward insurers, controlling rates to the point where it is unprofitable.

This strict regulation limits innovation in the business, but there are some things insurance companies can do to differentiate themselves. For example, by developing better computer systems and technology, the delivery of the product can be faster and less costly. Agents and brokers are eager to sell a company's product if they can offer fast service to their clients and improve their efficiency by having better systems to connect to.

Achieving Success

To be successful in the insurance industry, you have to continue to look for opportunities and develop relationships with others in the business. The insurance business is largely built on relationships.

Also, you cannot be afraid to take risks. You will not guess right every time, but if you guess right more times than you guess wrong, you will be a winner.

Utmost good faith is the golden rule in insurance. To define it further, you could say that having honest business practices is first, second is pricing the product fairly and third is paying claims properly. Honest business practices include dealing properly with all business partners, agents, brokers, re-insurers, employees and shareholders. Fair pricing means pricing each line of insurance so that a reasonable amount of profit is maintained to make sure the company is financially stable. Under-pricing to the point where a company is not financially stable does not help policyholders when a claim occurs and the company fails and cannot pay the claims. Finally, it is important to pay legitimate claims promptly and give good service, since that is why people buy insurance. At the same time, suspicious claims must be properly investigated because the payment of fraudulent losses ultimately increases the cost of insurance for all consumers.

Successful people are usually those who are able to make quick decisions and have a strong commitment to honor their obligations.

Changes and Trends in the Insurance Business

Governments are becoming more involved in regulating insurance products and premiums. However, the greatest challenge for the industry recently has been to find needed capital. From the late 1980s until 2000 the industry went through a "soft" market. In other words, investment income was high, so companies cut rates to obtain more business to have more money to invest. They did not concern themselves with underwriting profit. Interest rates dropped and companies started to become unprofitable. Some went out of business while others reduced their premium writings. Then the events of September 11, 2001 took place, with the destruction of the World Trade Center. In addition to the claims that resulted, the stock market dropped, leaving many insurers

99

with large investment losses. The worldwide capital of the insurance industry dropped from US$700 billion to US$550 billion in a period of less than a year. There was a market shortage and substantial premium increases, which was referred to as a "hard" market.

Looking forward, I expect to see the hard market with limited competition continue until interest rates increase. There will probably be a reduction in the number of individual insurance companies, as acquisitions and consolidations will take place. More financial organizations will develop one-stop centers to provide banking, mortgages, financial advice and insurance in one location. The big financial organizations will become bigger, while smaller ones will disappear.

William Star is chairman, president, and CEO of Kingsway Financial Services Inc. He started his insurance career in 1952 with the Kemper Group. In 1954, he joined the Gore Insurance Company and helped create a new Toronto branch. During that time he was an underwriter but also created a claims department in the branch.

After four years in the company ranks, he became an insurance broker and sold general and life insurance for seven years. In 1963, he returned to a company position and managed the Special Risks Division of Canadian General Insurance Company, now part of AVIVA. In 1967, he became the general manager of a British Columbia company, Pacific Automobile and Fire Insurance Company, and reorganized it in 1970 as an Ontario corporation, Pafco Insurance Company, now owned by Allstate. He later became president and purchased a 50 percent interest in the company. After a merger with an oil company, Pafco was sold, and Bill resigned in 1983 and joined York Fire and Casualty Insurance Company, now owned by Kingsway Financial.

In 1986, Bill spent four months with the Ontario Task Force on Insurance as an advisor. Later that year he created Kingsway General Insurance Company, an Ontario insurer that provides insurance for nonstandard automobiles, motorcycles, taxicabs, long-haul trucking, specialty property lines, bonds, marine cargo and other niche products. The company is licensed in every province and territory in Canada.

Kingsway Financial Services Inc. was created in 1989 and completed a public offering in December 1995. Kingsway's shares trade on the Toronto Stock Exchange and the New York Stock Exchange under the symbol KFS. The company now owns three insurance companies in Canada and six in the United States, with annual gross written premium income in excess of $2.6 billion.

Master the Basics

John W. Hayden
Chairman, President, & Chief Executive Officer
American Modern Insurance Group

The Theory Behind Insurance

The concept of insurance has changed from its original intent. Once it was the process of sharing or spreading *catastrophic* financial risk in order to protect an individual from financial ruin, through spreading the cost of a loss over the relative many, rather than to have it absorbed solely by the relative few.

The notion of catastrophic loss has somehow gotten distorted in more recent years, and people have come to expect *every* loss to be covered. The industry must to do a better job of positioning its coverage as "catastrophic protection against financial ruin," as opposed to "every loss is covered." If you look at the origins of the industry, that's really what it was all about. The creation of Lloyd's of London was to protect ship owners against the sinking of an individual ship. Ship owners all threw in, and if any one of them lost their ship, then everybody would pitch in to help cover the loss of the individual ship. The idea was really to spread the loss over the many versus the few. But as insurance companies have broadened coverage in recent years, they've done so with a mind toward protecting policyholders from most losses without achieving a sufficient increase in the premium rates they charge.

Insurance, when it does work, collects an adequate premium from the relative many to absorb the losses of the relative few. As policyholders, we buy insurance because we never know when something bad might happen to us. Insurers make money by producing a relatively modest margin on an underwriting basis and by investing the premiums collected in relatively conservative fixed return investment vehicles, in order to achieve part of their profits. The remainder of their profits needs to come from underwriting profit—paying out fewer dollars in losses and operating expenses than they take in, in the form of premiums.

The idea is that an insurance company makes money by providing a service to individuals who desire catastrophic financial protection. Insurance companies are able to achieve economies by providing that service to large numbers of people, rather than us, as individuals, having to absorb losses ourselves or go out and try to put together consortiums. Insurance companies are able to defray the ultimate cost of the insurance by generating a little bit of investment profit at the same time.

Achieving Differentiation

Companies can either be *the* low-cost provider in their chosen market (and there can only be one "low cost provider"), or they must differentiate themselves from their competition.   Some companies differentiate through advertising, by establishing a household brand name such as Allstate or State Farm.   That brand name allows them to be almost omnipresent.   Other companies differentiate themselves by offering coverage for unique or hard-to-place risks, and still others by providing superior service or by being easy to do business with.

Our company actually attempts to differentiate itself in all of these ways. We are not the low-cost provider in our chosen product lines nor in our chosen markets. We offer unique specialty personal lines products that others don't understand as well as we do. We bring those products to market through a variety of distribution channels. We service our products exceptionally well, both for our producing agency force as well as for the policyholder. We develop deep and enduring relationships with our business partners. And, ultimately, we differentiate ourselves by harnessing our data in these unusual product lines in such a way that we're better able to predict our results in these lines than can any of our competitors.

About Credibility

A company's track record reflects its credibility, stability through good markets and bad. Its customers, employees and business partners also reflect its credibility. Credibility is manifest in its ability to create enduring relationships; with customers—as is evidenced by high-customer retention rates—or with business partners, agencies, producers, associates and stock holders, as is evidenced by the tenure of these various relationships. The people who work in an organization have to believe in the company. Turnover rates in an organization are a particularly good indicator of credibility. People can't stay with a company forever if they don't believe it does business in a forthright and ethically appropriate kind of way.

Competing via Differentiation

Our company does not compete on the basis of price. We're not the low-cost provider, and our products are not the lowest-priced products. Chief among our differentiating points are our distribution strategies. For instance, in the manufactured housing business, we do business directly with mobile home dealers, mobile home finance companies and mobile home manufacturers. When they build, sell or finance a home, we encourage them to offer a little bit of our insurance on it. In so doing, we're capturing that business preemptively at what we call the "point of sale."

With respect to our agency-based business, we typically assume that a standard or direct writer is going to have a more competitive price than we do. Our pricing models are generally built assuming that business has found its way to us because it hasn't been successfully placed, for one underwriting reason or another, with a standard carrier. We're dealing with specialized distribution that takes all-comers; so, we price and design our products accordingly. We view distribution as our driving force, since we offer specialty or unique product lines in which the ultimate market potential is more limited than if we were to write homeowners' or automobile insurance. Therefore, we must achieve critical mass in our lines any way we can. We make our products available to customers in every way we can; then, we price and design our products in a way that is tailored to the business we are likely to receive from a particular channel of distribution.

Advertising isn't a big thing for our company. It's highly unlikely that we could ever achieve a retail brand name like Allstate or State Farm. We simply can't afford an advertising budget like that. However, we do have a good wholesale brand name. The agents know of our company; they know what specialty products we offer, and they know we are very good at what we do. We tend to target product lines where the agents have a tough time placing the business, so they know to turn to us in order to get it placed.

Establishing Rate Levels

Most of our products are template underwritten, which is to say that risks are not individually underwritten and priced. Our products are designed to fit a particular class of risk, identified on the basis of historical experience. We generally know the loss patterns of risks that are located in particular areas, whether they're more exposed to hurricanes or flood loss or heavy wind loss. We're also able to evaluate risk by the nature of the economy and geography in different territories. We design our products with a broad rating belt. We lay out prices so as to yield a pre-determined underwriting profit margin, predicated on our historical average experience for various risk profiles. We don't generally ask a lot of underwriting questions. Our assessment is predicated upon some pretty high-level data points about an individual and his or her property. We classify that risk according to a broad class rating approach.

Some people would suggest that, ultimately, there is an exact right rate for every risk. I don't agree. Picture two properties very similarly situated, similarly furnished, similarly maintained, occupied by very comparable families with very similar lifestyles, beliefs, values and the like. What is it, then, that causes one family to incur a loss and the other one not? Too often, after exhaustive analysis, it comes down to "luck of the draw." Once we come to understand this as insurers, it makes it easier for us to avoid over-analyzing or over-complicating risk. At the end of the day, it's as simple as dollars in versus dollars out. A company must take enough dollars in to have a reasonable amount left after covering its expenses and paying its claims.

Claims Management

Ultimately, a claim begins when an insured has a loss; when the insured has experienced some tragedy in his or her life. When policyholders incur a loss, if it's something devastating, like a hurricane, it may take them a couple of days before they even thinks to talk to their insurance agent or company. Typically the policyholder is going to report his or her loss quickly in the property insurance business. He or she is either going to report the loss directly to the insurance agent or to the company. This can be done over the telephone, via the mail or, increasingly now, the Internet. Our internal claims staff receives a notice of loss and assigns the loss to an adjuster for review. Our company handles 94 percent of our claims with our own staff, either by desk adjustment out of our home office or by a field claims settlement with one of our field staff adjusters that are located across the country. Since we offer specialty personal lines products, it's particularly important to us that we use our own staff. A manufactured home is not the same as a conventional home. Our adjusters need to understand the unique construction differences between the two and adjust the loss accordingly.

The loss is assigned to an adjuster, who is typically one of our employees but occasionally, where we don't have enough business to support a staff person, an independent third party. The adjuster then makes contact with the customer and arranges a time to get together and inspect the loss. The adjuster performs a loss assessment and begins to prepare an estimate of the damage. He or she applies the applicable coverage, terms and conditions and the policy deductible, if there is one, and arrange to pay the claim. In our case, we settle 90 percent of our claims within thirty days of when they are reported, and a great many of our claims are settled on our first contact with the insured. These are significant points of differentiation for our company vis-à-vis our competitors. A lot of companies write mobile home insurance, but few of them have staff adjusters who are uniquely trained in handling mobile home claims the way our people are.

Risk Assessment and Management

Risk varies by the class of business an insurer chooses to write. As a specialty personal lines insurer, our company's principal risks include fire, theft, liability and any number of different weather-related causes. Certainly there's a financial risk component to the insurance business. Investing in dangerous investment vehicles that fail to perform as expected would be a risk of another sort. But in terms of the insurable risk, it's principally the moral fiber of our policyholders and weather conditions. Understanding the moral fiber of our policyholders can assist us in predicting the ultimate risk profile of a particular insured. It can manifest itself in terms of an insured party's upkeep of its property, its insurance history, and its credit history.

Aside from the moral hazard, the physical condition and location of a property can also provide insight into the nature of a given risk. We can generally price for most of these factors. In much the same way as a life insurer can predict death rates from mortality tables, we can reasonably predict our losses based on the history of our book of business and the nature of the policyholder.

The one thing we can't predict is what Mother Nature is or isn't going to do to us in a given year. We do know, however, what she's done to us on average over time; so, we build our premium rate levels and our business forecasts based on historical weather loss averages. When weather is better than average, we benefit, and when it's worse than average, we come up short. When we benefit, it's reflected in our premium rate levels, either in the form of rate decreases or in the form of lesser rate increases. When we come up short, likewise, it's reflected in our premium rate levels in the form of increased rates to absorb the impact of excessive weather. Weather can include anything from tornadoes to floods, hurricanes, snowstorms, ice storms and more. We insure a lot of manufactured housing and low-valued housing, principally, property risks. When Mother Nature decides to get ugly, it impacts our book of business. We tend to live with the Weather Channel in the spring and summer months.

Profitability

All products, if they're properly designed and priced, should produce a reasonable return. Some companies subscribe to the bigger risk, bigger return theory. They price more exotic products to yield a significant profit in years where there isn't a loss, but they run the risk of absorbing a potentially very significant loss when one does occur. I'll use as an example, insuring the space shuttle. The odds are pretty strong that there isn't going to be an accident, but if there is an accident it's going to be catastrophic in nature. Insuring that risk is a daunting process. There isn't a lot of experience to base one's underwriting and risk pricing on. Some markets will say, "Sure, we'll insure that," and they'll just throw a high price on the cost of the insurance, because there's no way to know what the real cost is. If there's no loss, then they realize a handsome profit. If there is a loss, it will take them years to make up for it. However, since such companies tend to write a lot of unusual risks like this, the law of large numbers tends to work out for them.

Our business is not nearly so exotic. We try to manage our business to yield a 15 percent return on beginning equity, on average, over time. Some years we'll come up short of that objective, and other years we might exceed it. But we're pricing our products to produce a reasonable return. We're factoring into the pricing of those products our typical investment yields, our cost of doing business, including our operating costs and the acquisition costs associated with our business, and our historical loss patterns. The insurance industry has often failed to produce an acceptable profit margin relative to other industries, because it's failed in its efforts to properly match the premium rates it charges, with the coverage it provides, with the losses that develop from that coverage.

When you look for the biggest moneymakers for the industry, it isn't any particular product line, and it isn't any particular investment strategy. It's companies that really pay attention to the details of their business and execute effectively. These are the companies that are able to achieve satisfactory returns over time.

Clearly, investment income is a significant piece of the insurance operating equation. Insurance companies are required to invest conservatively so that they're able to turn investments into cash quickly if cash is needed to pay claims. However, investing is one of the primary ways in which insurers can deliver value to their policyholders. By investing premiums so as to ensure a positive investment return, insurers can ultimately afford to charge policyholders less and still achieve a reasonable profit. Producing a profit *is* desirable; too often today, public skepticism and cynicism seems to suggest that profit is a bad thing. However, without the profit motive, companies have no incentive to exist. Shareholders have no motivation to invest. The result is that job creation grinds to a halt. The profit motive is critical. The value that insurance companies have to bring is that they can spread the risks of the relative few across the relative many, and they can do it more efficiently than we, as individuals, can. They operate efficiently, and they're able to offset some of their operating costs and satisfy some of their profit objectives by combining their investment returns with their underwriting margins. Insurance companies can provide a much needed and mutually beneficial service to society.

Insurance companies can make money in ways beyond simply selling policies to customers in the hope of generating an underwriting profit and aside from investing the funds in order to produce positive investment returns. Insurance companies can also outsource certain unique service capabilities to other companies on a fee-for-service basis. They can provide non-insurance ancillary services to common customers. By way of example, we do a lot of business with large financial institutions. Financial institutions are in the business of making loans; they're not necessarily in the business of tracking the insurance on the collateral on those loans, but they have an insurable interest in that collateral. So, we've developed an insurance tracking service where we charge the financial institution a fee per loan per month to track the status of insurance on their loan collateral. If the collateral goes uninsured, then we communicate with the customer and remind the customer of the obligation to maintain insurance on the collateral satisfactory to the lender. If, ultimately, the customer fails to do so, then we'll place insurance on that risk and charge it to the loan.

We also, from time to time—because we're active in these specialty product lines, where others lack our expertise—outsource our unique claims capabilities. Additionally, we will take our capabilities to other insurance companies who want to be able to offer their agents our product lines but don't necessarily have the in-house expertise to do so themselves.

Challenges of Working in the Insurance Industry

Like all industries, the insurance industry has a terminology all its own. This can really complicate things. It creates a mystique and a confusion surrounding the industry, which can result in a certain amount of consumer distrust. It doesn't help that we're actually required to keep two sets of books in the insurance industry. Most people are familiar with GAAP accounting. Few people understand statutory accounting, which is the regulatory standard of the insurance industry. An insurance regulator or rating agency's primary job is to be sure that policyholders will be compensated in the event of a loss. They, therefore, want to make sure there are sufficient assets available to pay all legitimate claims in the event of a serious occurrence. Statutory accounting is designed to facilitate such critical analysis. Nevertheless, the fact that we are required to keep a second set of books in the insurance industry is confusing.

Our industry is complicated on so many levels. It's complicated by state regulation. There is considerable debate over whether insurance should be regulated at the federal level or at the state level, as is currently the case. In the property/casualty insurance business, every state is unique in terms of its risk characteristics. Some states are coastal and are, therefore, more vulnerable to hurricanes and other unique occurrences; other states are flood or tornado prone; others have depressed economies. Regulating these factors on a federal level is, I think, difficult at best. Licensing laws requiring that producers are properly trained and licensed to represent insurance transactions to policyholders could, conceivably, be effectively managed at the federal level. Today's state regulation does tend to complicate such matters.

Rating agencies are another complicating factor in the insurance business. Their objectives are centered on protecting policyholders in the event of an absolute loss. The confusion that can result from their ratings, which may or may not reflect the ultimate financial stability of a company in all circumstances, is another complicating factor.

And then, finally, I think another entity that complicates our business is the plaintiff's bar. Frivolous lawsuits can drive up the cost of insurance considerably, either through the escalation of an insurance company's defense costs or through the payment of illegitimate losses, losses without any apparent merit that are, for one reason or another, determined to be payable

Maintaining Company Culture and Vision

A company's culture, and its ability to align and collaborate around a widely shared vision, is central to its ultimate success. We fundamentally believe this is the key point of differentiation for our organization.

We maintain seven operating principles:

- We focus on specialty insurance products where, although there may be competition, it's competition that's not necessarily focused on each of our product lines.
- We maintain a diverse distribution platform; so, we'll take our products to market in just about every way you can fathom.
- We master the claims process around the unusual product lines in which we operate
- We deploy a multiple company structure to tailor-make our products to the channel of distribution from which the business emanates.
- We maintain an underwriting discipline and focus in each of the product lines we offer.
- We'll manage our concentrations of exposure carefully so that no single event can devastate us.
- We'll develop systems that will allow us to effectively execute our business strategy.

I believe that the one constant in business is change, and the only way that you can position yourself to continually adapt to change is to have a clear sense of purpose, a clear set of operating principles, a clear mission and vision and a succinct and widely shared set of corporate values that allow you to shut out all of the noise and allow your team to stay focused on the business at hand. These tools allows us to align ourselves around our jobs, take in the feedback that we get about changing circumstances around us and position our business plan properly to achieve ongoing success.

We have three ultimate strategic objectives: profit, growth and people. Profit is the be all and end all. Without it, none of us has much else to worry about. If we get profit right, then growth is a good thing. If we get profit wrong, then growth can be a dangerous thing. We really aren't going to achieve either growth or profit without a team of people who understand the mission, who are positioned properly and are playing to their strengths, who have a clear sense of what it is we need them to do, who get clear feedback about the job they're doing and who have the tools they need to get the job done.

I think success isn't always measured in terms of an absolute return on equity. There are years that are exceptionally good, and there are years that are exceptionally bad, through no fault or through no great gift of ours but, rather, just because of the luck of the draw. The ultimate measure of success is the ability of an organization to effectively perpetuate its culture and continue to exist as a viable service provider, in the future as it has in the past.

Innovation in the Insurance Business

One of our values is creativity, and the tag line that follows it is 'You better find a new way of doing it tomorrow, because yesterday's way ain't gonna be good enough anymore."

Insurance isn't rocket science, and there are far more creative people in the world that are doing really phenomenal things. There are far more creative people in the world than would typically populate an insurance company, myself included. But we do have to always be thinking about the changes occurring in the marketplace around us, in the world around us and in our customers' lives that we need to be properly responsive to. The challenge for a company like ours, I think, is to innovate in a methodical kind of way, in an evolutionary kind of way, as opposed to a revolutionary.

Some companies thrive on revolution, on really being out on the bleeding edge and coming up with new ideas. But I believe that the vast majority of business is conducted at the 100-course level and that very little of it is actually occurring at the 400-course level, or at a level that is strategic in nature. Succeeding at the 100-course level involves communication, alignment and collaboration around a relative few initiatives. All organizations have finite resources, and they must allocate those resources in such a way as to actually accomplish a few good things. In our scheme of things, innovation involves taking relatively moderate baby-steps to make our products more responsive to changing circumstances in the market.

Years ago, I heard and adopted the following adage, which I think best summarizes innovation in the insurance business: "If you have data and you do nothing with it, it remains data. However, if you take that data, and you add a little bit of learning to it, it becomes information. Then, if you take that information, and you add a little bit more learning to it, it becomes knowledge. And if you take that knowledge, and you add a little bit more learning to it, it becomes wisdom."

If you read through the documentation that is the cornerstone of our organization, we talk about drawing on the collective wisdom of our team. The ability to retain people, to have high associate retention rates, to have turnover rates that are low, allows us to build the collective wisdom within our team. While employee retention is a good thing, zero turnover is not. We monitor, for instance, our desirable vs. undesirable turnover. Our overall turnover is in the single digits, but we actually encourage some of that turnover by telling people, "This may not be the job for you." So the real key, if we're going to draw on the collective wisdom of the team, is making sure that we're holding on to the right people and giving them the right resources necessary to perpetuate and share their wisdom effectively throughout the organization. I think that's really central to innovation. Too often, I see companies that commit the same mistakes over and over and over again. Often times, it's a different group of people making the same mistake. In our case, we're trying to hold on to that strong nucleus of people that allows us to develop the wisdom that causes us, hopefully, to repeat fewer of our mistakes.

Recent Changes and the Future of Insurance

I think all businesses, all industries, are changing constantly, and the key is to keep your business relatively simple in the face of all those changes. Clearly, globalism is an enormous change in all our lives. No business can say that it is not global in nature anymore. Even though our primary business is conducted within the United States, we do business with re-insurers located around the globe. More and more, we find ourselves investigating opportunities beyond our borders. So globalism is one key change.

Coastal development is another big change. Back in the fifties, there just weren't that many luxury homes located along the coastline in the United States. Today, it is the dream of many Americans. There's been a dramatic increase in the dollar value of exposures that are concentrated within ten miles of the U.S. coastline.

Terrorism is obviously a significant wake up call in the last several years, domestically in the wake of 9/11 and globally for, probably, the last two decades. The United States has just been a little bit slower waking up to it. But these factors are always there.

The other change that is real is the cost and pace of technological evolution. Being able to keep up with the latest and greatest changes in technology and leveraging those innovations effectively into one's business without spending yourself out of existence is really a tremendous challenge. I think the way you deal with that is just to keep it as simple as you possibly can. Measure every step you take along the way against each one of those changing dynamics.

The future holds more of the same. The only constant in life is change. I think the key is to build an organization that can adapt easily and effectively to change. The more likely it becomes that you can achieve organizational alignment, the more you can adapt effectively to changing circumstances. Competitive pressures are constant; they may be slightly different tomorrow than they were yesterday, but they're going to be just as real tomorrow as they were yesterday. In our case, we're a specialty/niche player, and we have to constantly re-evaluate and re-justify our niches. We must be mindful of the changing landscape around us and of how we're positioned within it.

I'd love to see the industry adopt true pricing discipline, where competitive pressures didn't get in the way of charging an appropriate rate for a risk. All too often in this industry, people can't resist the temptation to grow their business by cutting their rates. The result is the hard market swings and soft market swings we've endured over the years. Our company operates in lines of business where we don't fluctuate with the market. We're probably the only insurance company in North America that can say that it has raised its rates every year for the last twenty years. We don't compete on price. Nevertheless, the fluctuating market conditions do tend to impact our results, in spite of the fact that we don't give into market pricing pressure. I'd love to see the industry develop real pricing discipline and stick to it, so that we could level out some of these dramatic cycle swings. Doing so would substantially enhance the insurance industry's credibility with the public.

Words of Wisdom

I find myself most often advising people to breathe. Too often, we make things more complicated than they need to be. By mastering small component tasks, we can keep the overall task simpler. The simpler we keep it, the easier it is to breathe. And the easier it is to breathe, the more likely it is that we can all understand how our individual responsibilities contribute toward common objectives and experience mutual success and, ultimately, have fun doing it. I know it sounds overly simplistic, but too often people stop breathing, and when they stop breathing, they stop thinking. I think breathing is number one.

Number two is to be a constant student of your business. I read a lot. I read a lot about everything, probably fifty or more periodicals a week. I read a lot about technology. Even still, my wife and children will tell you I'm a techno-idiot. While I may not know a bit from a byte, I actually do have a clear sense for where we want to take technology in our organization, not because I understand how to program it, but because I understand how it fits strategically with where we're going. I make myself study that. So breathing and learning and reading, I think, are three musts.

Finally, and perhaps most importantly, I've been taught that every day you either get better or you get worse; you do not stay the same. So, every night, I try to go to bed a little bit better off for having worked that day to be better than I was when I woke up that morning.

Mr. Hayden is President and Chief Executive Officer of The Midland Company, a Cincinnati, Ohio-based specialty property/casualty insurance company. Midland's insurance operations do business as the American Modern Insurance Group. Mr. Hayden also serves as American Modern's

Chairman, President, and Chief Executive Officer. Midland trades publicly on the NASDAQ National Market under ticker symbol "MLAN." The Company's current market capitalization is approximately $450 million.

American Modern is widely recognized as an industry leader in providing manufactured housing insurance. The Company also writes motorcycle, watercraft, dwelling fire, recreational vehicle and collectible car insurance through its extensive agency network, in addition to credit life, collateral protection and mortgage fire insurance in support of its many financial institution partners.

A + rated by A.M. Best, American Modern has consistently produced superior financial results. The Company has achieved a ten-year average statutory combined ratio of 97.5 percent and has produced a ten-year average compound annual premium growth rate of 11.8 percent. Today, the company serves nearly one and a half million policyholders.

Midland posted net income for the twelve months ended December 31, 2003 of $23.3 million, $1.30 per on revenues of $718.2 million. The company's total assets are $1.2 billion, and its shareholder's equity reached a record $356.1 million as of December 31, 2003. Midland's track record of producing consistently superior financial results is largely responsible for the company being named one of America's "200 Best Small Companies" by Forbes Magazine in October, 2001.

Mr. Hayden joined Midland/American Modern in June of 1981 after receiving his MBA from Miami University. He completed his undergraduate studies at Northwestern University in June, 1979. He has served on Midland's Board of Directors since 1991.

In addition to his duties at Midland, Mr. Hayden serves on the Board of Directors of Ohio National Financial Services; the Advisory Board for U.S.

Bancorp in Cincinnati, Ohio; the Board of Trustees of The Greater Cincinnati Chamber of Commerce and the Board of Governors of The Metropolitan Club. In addition, he is a member of The Center for Quality of Management, The Commercial Club, The Recreation Roundtable and Young President's Organization.

Mr. Hayden and his wife Carrie reside in Cincinnati, Ohio and have three children, John Jr., Kate and Abbey.

Other Best Sellers

Visit Your Local Bookseller Today or www.Aspatore.com For A Complete Title List

- <u>Ninety-Six and Too Busy to Die</u> - Life Beyond the Age of Dying - $24.95

- <u>Technology Blueprints</u> - Strategies for Optimizing and Aligning Technology Strategy and Business - $69.95

- <u>The CEO's Guide to Information Availability</u> - Why Keeping People and Information Connected is Every Leader's New Priority - $27.95

- <u>Being There Without Going There</u> - Managing Teams Across Time Zones, Locations and Corporate Boundaries - $24.95

- <u>Profitable Customer Relationships</u> - CEOs from Leading Software Companies on using Technology to Maximize Acquisition, Retention and Loyalty - $27.95

- <u>The Entrepreneurial Problem Solver</u> - Leading CEOs on How to Think Like an Entrepreneur and Solve Any Problem for Your Team/Company - $27.95

- <u>The Philanthropic Executive</u> - Establishing a Charitable Plan for Individuals and Businesses - $27.95

- <u>The Golf Course Locator for Business Professionals</u> - Organized by Closest to Largest 500 Companies, Cities and Airports - $12.95

- <u>Living Longer Working Stronger</u> - 7 Steps to Capitalizing on Better Health - $14.95

- <u>Business Travel Bible</u> - Must Have Phone Numbers, Business Resources, Maps and Emergency Info - $19.95

- <u>ExecRecs</u> - Executive Recommendations for the Best Business Products and Services Professionals Use to Excel - $14.95

Call 1-866-Aspatore or Visit <u>www.Aspatore.com</u> to Order